FOOD, WINE, & FRIENDS

FOOD, WINE, & FRIENDS

simple menus for great entertaining

FIONA BECKETT

photography by Peter Cassidy

RYLAND
PETERS
& SMALL
LONDON NEW YORK

Dedication
For Will and Maria

First published in the USA in 2007
by Ryland Peters & Small, Inc.
519 Broadway, 5th Floor
New York, NY 10012
www.rylandpeters.com

10 9 8 7 6 5 4 3 2 1

Printed and bound in China.

Library of Congress Cataloging-in-Publication Data

Beckett, Fiona.
  Food, wine, & friends / Fiona Beckett ; photography
by Peter Cassidy.
     p. cm.
  Includes index.
  ISBN 978-1-84597-465-7
  1. Cookery. 2. Entertaining. I. Cassidy, Peter. II.
Title.
  TX715.B393 2007
  641.5--dc22

                              2007017247

Design and Photographic Art Direction
  Steve Painter
Editor Julia Charles
Production Gemma Moules
Publishing Director Alison Starling

Food Stylist Annie Rigg
Prop Stylist Helen Trent
Indexer Hilary Bird

Notes
• All spoon measurements are level, unless
otherwise stated.
• Eggs are medium unless otherwise specified.
Please note that the recipes on pages 25, 42, 95, and
119 contain raw eggs. Uncooked or partially cooked
eggs should not be served to the very old, frail,
young children, pregnant women, or those with
compromised immune systems.
• Ovens should be preheated to the specified
temperature. Recipes in this book were tested using
a regular oven. If using a fan-assisted oven, follow
the manufacturer's instructions for adjusting
temperatures.
• All herbs used in these recipes are fresh unless
otherwise specified.

contents

the menus

how wine can enhance your enjoyment of food

Food, wine, and friends. Can there be a better formula for an evening's entertainment? No one element is as good in isolation. Friends without food or wine: good to see them, but it can all seem rather rushed. Food without wine or friends: functional rather than fun. Wine without food or friends simply isn't as enjoyable at all.

Countries where wine is a part of life, like France and Italy, know this instinctively. The wine goes on the table automatically—they know the food tastes better as a result. It helps relax your guests and aids digestion, helping you to savor each mouthful more intensely. Sipping wine slows down the pace of the meal.

It also—and this hasn't yet fully been recognized—helps the busy host or hostess make an impact with their entertaining. If you've bought a ready-made or take-out meal (as so many of us do these days), your guests will more than likely be aware of that (after all, they do it too!.) But if you choose an intriguing wine or other drink to serve with it—one that is not only interesting in its own right but heightens the flavor of the food, then you'll have created an experience to remember.

The beauty of this approach is that you don't have to be an experienced cook to pull it off. You simply need to develop a flair for what ingredients work well together, just as those who dress stylishly can put together a "look" or others can make their house look great by the colors and furnishings they choose.

This book is very much written with the pressures of modern life in mind. We want to show our friends hospitality, but we simply don't have time in our busy days to make everything from scratch. So we need to be more imaginative and flexible about the way we do it.

Don't feel duty bound to offer a full meal. Sure, it's fun occasionally to throw a full-blown dinner party such as my Fine Wine Dinner (see page 130), but it's equally enjoyable to just invite friends round for a few tapas (see page 66) or for margaritas and a few tostaditas (see page 62.) Or ask them to come round after dinner for an indulgent dessert and a glass of sweet wine (see the Just Desserts section from page 140.) They'll love the novelty and, faced with far less work in the kitchen, so will you!

Why not try reflecting the seasons in your choice of food and drink. You'll also make life easier for yourself and more enjoyable for your guests. Let local food growers and producers inspire you with the first of the new season's organic vegetables and throw together a Farmers' Market Supper (see page 78.) At the end of the year, make an old-fashioned Vegetarian Harvest Supper (see page 96) with the pick of the fall's produce.

When the weather heats up, take your lead from those who live year-round in a tropical climate and serve spicy but cooling food (see page 72.) When temperatures hit zero, stay indoors and huddle up around the comforting sort of food I've suggested in my It's Cold Outside menu (see page 102.) Even the cheeseboards you serve your guests can be given an imaginative seasonal twist, as you'll see from my ideas on pages 136–139.

I suggest that you use the menus and ideas in this book as a starting point for a new style of entertaining at home—one where the idea comes first, then you invite friends round to share the experience, rather than inviting them round then desperately wondering what to cook for them.

Cook if you feel like it, buy in food if you really don't. Use interesting and carefully chosen drinks—beers, cocktails, juices, and liqueurs—as well as wine, to make your meals special. Most importantly, relax and enjoy!

the secrets of successful entertaining

For many people entertaining is stressful: something to be crammed into an already hectic life. We invite friends, work colleagues, or neighbours round on impulse, then wish we hadn't. We leave thinking about the event until the last minute, try something too complicated, then panic. But it really doesn't need to be like that. Just follow these simple tips and enjoy rather than endure the events you host:

DO

• Match the occasion to the guests...

There's no point in inviting older family members or friends to a noisy stand-up drinks party where they struggle to hear who they're talking to. They'd much rather be seated in a smaller group around the table. Younger friends on the other hand will be perfectly happy to eat finger food and perch a plate on their knee.

•...and the time of year.

Seasonal food is so much more inviting—light, fresh food in the summer warm, comforting food when it's miserable and cold. Have a Plan B if it's an outdoor event—you can never be a hundred percent sure of the weather.

• Plan ahead. Make a couple of dishes in advance and freeze them. Make sure you have the equipment you need, especially if you're catering for a crowd (see page 147.) Draw up a full shopping list and get as much as possible done the day beforehand.

• Rope in friends to help. If they offer to help with the cooking, accept gratefully—letting them know the kind of dish you'd like if there's a theme to the event. If there's a task to be done on the day—grilling, juicing, making cocktails—get them involved.

• If you cheat (as we all do from time to time), cheat in style! Pretty-up store-bought food and give it a personal touch, adding fresh herbs, or a squeeze of lemon juice.

• Lay on plenty of water and other soft drinks in addition to the alcohol.

DON'T

• Invite people you don't know too well for a long evening. Ask them round for drinks so they can stay for as long, or as short, a time as they like and talk to a range of people.

• Host a huge party if organization isn't your strong suit. Hold two or three smaller events rather than one big one or get it catered by someone else

• Feel guilty about not making every single thing yourself. The menus that follow in this book contain dishes that will work well together, but you can always buy a similar dish.

• Tackle a complicated recipe you've never made before. If you feel unsure about it, try it out on the family first. Never attempt a whole menu of untried dishes if you're not a confident cook.

• Worry about impressing your guests. Your friends come to see you, not to judge how your table is decorated or how good a cook you are—at least that's what real friends do. If you have to offer hospitality to someone who stresses you out, invite them to a restaurant rather than to your home.

• Spend all your time locked away in the kitchen or jumping up and down at the table. Get ahead, then relax and enjoy yourself on the day. (There's no point in entertaining if you don't!)

• Top up glasses too regularly. Both you and your guests will feel uncomfortable if they drink too much.

food and wine matching made easy

If you've ever tasted a food you love with a wine that matches it perfectly, you'll know that the combination of the two can be even better than the food and wine on its own. But how to find those perfect pairings? The old "white wine with fish, red wine with meat" rule is a bit dated, as anyone who has enjoyed a seared tuna steak with a Pinot Noir well knows. Wine has changed. Food has changed. The only rule is that there are no hard and fast rules, just combinations that most people are likely to enjoy.

Basically, there's no great mystique about it. Simply use your existing knowledge of food and think of wine as another ingredient you have to take into account when you're planning a meal—as you would when you choose a vegetable or sauce to serve on the side. The more food and wine matches you try, the more confident you'll feel, so take every opportunity to try out different combinations, particularly in restaurants that serve wines by the glass or suggest food and wine pairings with their menu. Here are some simple pointers that may help you:

• Match the wine to the sauce, not the basic ingredient. Chicken, for example, can be cooked in any number of different ways, so it's more useful to think about whether it's served in a creamy white wine and mushroom sauce (a smooth, dry white), a red wine sauce like *coq au vin* (a similar wine to the one you use to cook it), a Thai green curry sauce (a fruity, off-dry white), or a barbecue sauce or marinade (a ripe, fruity red).

• Think about the temperature and intensity of the dish. Dishes that are served raw or delicate, steamed dishes need lighter wines (usually white) than ones that are roasted, seared or grilled (more often red.) Homemade dishes will often be more intensely seasoned than store-bought ones, so may need more intensely flavored wines.

• Take into account what else is on the plate. Strongly flavored vegetables, such as asparagus, red cabbage, or beet or fruity salsas and relishes, can make a difference to the wine you choose. If you served broiled salmon with asparagus, for instance, you'd probably go for a Sauvignon Blanc, while if you made a spicy mango salsa to go with it, go for a Semillion or Semillion-Chardonnay, or a fruity red.

• If you're serving several wines during a meal, you should generally start with lighter, drier wines and move on to richer, more full-bodied ones. Usually, that means white followed by red, but you could easily serve a full-bodied white with a main course or a lighter red followed by a more full-bodied one.

• Dessert wines need to be sweeter than the food they're accompanying, otherwise they can taste sharp.

• Stuck? Imagine wine as a fruit. If it's light and citrussy, it will go with dishes where you might think of adding a squeeze of lemon as you would to fried fish or chicken. If it has ripe red berry fruit flavors, it will probably go with ingredients to which you might think of adding red fruits such as duck, turkey, or lamb.

For more information on this topic, see Matching Wine to Food (page 150) and Matching Food to Wine (page 153) or look at my website www.matchingfoodandwine.com

the menus

friends for brunch

menu for 6

On weekends it's good to change the usual workday routine of breakfast and lunch and offer brunch, especially if you have guests staying over. The food needs to be light and fresh but flavorful, healthy but comforting. A main course of kedgeree is easier than juggling a fry-up for a crowd, while the muffins can be made in advance, frozen, and lightly reheated. And the juice bar makes a fun focus to the occasion.

Bloody Mary granitas

summer berries with Greek yogurt, honey, and granola

smoked salmon kedgeree

mini-muffins:

banana and honey; bacon, onion, and cheddar;

zucchini, goat cheese, and scallion

"Juice Bar"
St. Clement's punch, strawberry sunrise

TO DRINK: Sparkling wine is the best wine to serve at a brunch: it suits the time of day perfectly and is a great match with eggs. Unless it's a special occasion, it needn't be Champagne: there are many good quality sparkling wines from Australia, California, and New Zealand. You can serve it straight or mix it half and half with fresh orange juice for a refreshing Bucks Fizz. I'd also lay on a few beers (golden lagers or wheat beers) for those who prefer beer to wine.

Bloody Mary granitas

A refreshing palate cleanser to kick off or round up brunch.

7–8 tomatoes, skinned and roughly chopped

2 cups tomato juice

3½ fl oz. vodka

1 tablespoon Worcestershire sauce

freshly squeezed juice of 1 lime

1 teaspoon celery salt

1 teaspoon finely grated onion

sea salt, freshly ground black pepper, and hot pepper sauce, such as Tabasco, to taste

a few finely snipped chives, to garnish

Makes 10–12 shots

Put the tomatoes in a food processor and whizz until smooth. Add the tomato juice and vodka and whizz again. Next, add the Worcestershire sauce, lime juice, celery salt, and onion, whizz, then check the seasoning, adding salt, pepper, and hot pepper sauce to taste. Pour into a shallow freezerproof container and freeze for about 1½ hours. Rough up the surface with a fork and freeze for another 45 minutes. Fork through again and freeze for another 45 minutes if serving straight away or freeze until hard if making ahead, in which case mellow in the fridge for 30 minutes before serving.

Spoon into shot glasses and garnish with a few finely snipped chives. Serve with coffee spoons or other small spoons.

summer berries with Greek yogurt, honey, and granola

Fill a large glass bowl with assorted fresh berries such as strawberries, raspberries, blueberries, and stoned cherries. Have a big bowl of Greek or Greek-style yogurt and a smaller one of Greek honey or other flavored honey alongside, together with a bowl of crunchy granola.

smoked salmon kedgeree

Kedgeree is an Anglo-Indian dish that stems from the days of the Raj. This party version is based on a relatively new product—lightly smoked salmon, which gives it a particularly luxurious flavor. If you can't find it, use organic salmon and add a little bit of smoked salmon at the end when you add the shrimp.

3 large eggs

8 oz. undyed skinless, smoked haddock or cod fillet

8 oz. lightly smoked skinless, salmon fillet or ordinary salmon fillet

3 tablespoons sunflower oil

1 onion, finely chopped

2–3 teaspoons mild curry powder

1½ cups basmati rice

6 oz. cooked shelled shrimp

3 tablespoons butter, softened

2–3 tablespoons freshly squeezed lemon juice

3 heaping tablespoons chopped cilantro leaves, plus a few whole leaves to garnish

sea salt and freshly ground black pepper

Serves 6

Bring a small saucepan of water to a boil. Prick the eggs if you have an egg pricker, lower them carefully into the water and boil for 10–12 minutes. Drain off the water, pour cold running water over the eggs, then let cool in cold water.

Put the smoked haddock and salmon into a large saucepan and pour over just enough cold water to cover. Bring gradually to a boil, then once the water is bubbling, take the pan off the heat and cover it with a lid or a piece of foil. Leave for 5 minutes, then carefully remove the fish fillets. Pour 2½ cups of the cooking water into a jug and set aside.

Heat the oil in another heavy pan or flameproof casserole and fry the onion over moderate heat for about 6–7 minutes until starting to turn dark brown at the edges. Sprinkle in the curry powder (I use 3 teaspoons, but use 2 if you want a slightly milder flavor.) Add the rice, stir again and pour in the reserved water you used for cooking the fish. Bring to a boil then turn the heat right down and cover the pan. Cook for about 15–20 minutes until all the liquid has been absorbed.

Meanwhile, shell and quarter the eggs. Set aside 6 quarters and roughly chop the rest. Flake the fish, being very careful to remove any remaining bones. Once the rice is cooked, fork it through and tip in the cooked fish, shrimp, and chopped eggs, cover the pan and leave for 5 minutes over very low heat. Turn off the heat, add the butter, fork through. Season to taste with the lemon juice and a little salt and pepper if you think it needs it and fork through the chopped cilantro. Serve on a warmed platter garnished with the quartered eggs and the remaining cilantro leaves.

* You can keep the kedgeree warm in a covered pan for about 15–20 minutes before serving or transfer it to a very low oven for about 30–40 minutes.

breakfast muffins

banana and honey mini-muffins

3 tablespoons unsalted butter

2 tablespoons clear honey

1 heaping tablespoon plain yogurt

about ¼ cup milk

½ teaspoon pure vanilla extract

1 cup plus 2 tablespoons all-purpose flour

1½ teaspoons baking powder

½ teaspoon ground cinnamon

¼ teaspoon salt

1 large egg, lightly beaten

1 medium-ripe banana

superfine sugar, for topping

a 12-cup small muffin or tartlet pan
12 small paper cases

Makes about 12 small muffins

Preheat the oven to 375°F. Line the cups in the pan with the paper cases. Gently heat the butter in a saucepan with the honey. Set aside and cool slightly. Put the yogurt in a measuring cup and mix in enough milk to bring it to just over the ⅓ cup mark. Stir in the vanilla extract. Sift the flour into a bowl with the baking powder, cinnamon, and salt and hollow out a dip in the center. Pour the honey and butter mixture, beaten egg, and yogurt and milk into the flour and mix in lightly and swiftly with a large metal spoon to get a rough batter. (Don't overmix—it doesn't have to be completely smooth.) Peel the banana, slice it thinly into the batter and fold in lightly so that all the slices are coated. Spoon the batter into the muffin cases and sprinkle each with a little superfine sugar. Bake for about 20 minutes or until fully risen and well browned. Transfer to a wire rack and eat as soon as cool enough to handle.

bacon, onion, and cheddar mini-muffins

1 tablespoon sunflower or other vegetable oil

2½ oz. cubed pancetta or bacon

1 small onion, finely chopped

3 tablespoons unsalted butter

1 heaping tablespoon plain yogurt

about ¼ cup milk

1 cup plus 2 tablespoons all-purpose flour

1½ teaspoons baking powder

¼ teaspoon salt

2 tablespoons finely grated Parmesan cheese

1 large egg, lightly beaten

⅓ cup coarsely grated cheddar cheese

a 12-cup small muffin or tartlet pan
12 small paper cases

Makes about 12 small muffins

Preheat the oven to 375°F. Line the cups in the pan with the paper cases. Heat the oil in a small skillet and fry the bacon for a couple of minutes until it starts to brown. Add the onion, stir and cook over low to medium heat for another 5 minutes until the onion is soft, then set aside to cool. Gently melt the butter in another pan and leave to cool. Put the yogurt in a measuring cup and mix in enough milk to bring it to just over the ⅓ cup mark. Sift the flour into a bowl with the baking powder and salt. Add the Parmesan and hollow out a dip in the center. Pour the beaten egg, melted butter, and yogurt and milk into the flour and mix in lightly and swiftly with a large metal spoon to get a rough batter. (Don't overmix—it doesn't have to be completely smooth.) Fold in the bacon and onion. Spoon the batter into the muffin cases and sprinkle each with a little grated cheddar. Bake for 20–25 minutes or until fully risen and well browned. Transfer to a wire rack and eat as soon as cool enough to handle.

zucchini, goat cheese, and scallion mini-muffins

Follow the Bacon, Onion, and Cheddar Mini-Muffin recipe substituting ½ cup grated zucchini, ½ cup grated firm goat cheese and 1–2 trimmed and thinly sliced scallions for the bacon, onion, and cheddar. (You don't need to precook the zucchini and onion, so you don't need the oil either.) Again, save some of the cheese for topping the muffins.

You could also add a tablespoon of snipped fresh dill to the mixture. I think these are better served cold rather than warm.

juice bar

It's fun to give your guests a chance to make their own smoothies and juices. Just set out a selection of different fruits and a blender or juicer. Combinations that go well are all kinds of citrus fruits; strawberries, orange and banana; and carrot, apple, lemon, and ginger. (See also Watermelon and Strawberry cooler page 49.)

Time-saving tip:

If you don't have a juicer, buy premium ready-made chilled juices or smoothies and serve them in attractive glass pitchers.

St. Clement's punch

This is a fresh, zesty, citrus-based punch that's packed with vitamin C.

1 cup freshly squeezed orange juice (about 4 oranges)
²/₃ cup freshly squeezed pink grapefruit juice (1–2 grapefruit)
1 cup traditional lemonade, chilled
slices of orange and lemon, to garnish

Serves 4–6

Simply pour the orange and pink grapefruit juice into a pitcher, top up with the lemonade and stir well. Add a few slices of orange and lemon to the pitcher and serve.

* If you're feeling indulgent, simply add a tablespoon of Grand Marnier liqueur. It just gives it that extra edge!

strawberry sunrise

Technically, this is a smoothie (a mixture of fruit juice and yogurt) rather than a juice and can be made in an ordinary blender. Ideal for those who can't face solid food until lunchtime.

2 ripe bananas
1 cup fresh strawberries
freshly squeezed juice of 2 oranges
1¼ cups plain yogurt
clear honey, to taste

Serves 2–3

Peel and slice the banana. Hull and halve the strawberries. Place both in a blender goblet with the juice of 1 orange and whizz until smooth. Add the yogurt and honey to taste and whizz again.

an Italian al fresco lunch

menu for 6

Combine an Italian menu with eating out of doors, and you have a guaranteed formula for happy guests. It's easy on the cook too. The Ham and Melon Platter couldn't be simpler to put together and, with its pale green, orange, and pink colors, makes a strikingly pretty plate to bring to the table. The Grape and Mascarpone Tart takes very little time to assemble—so all you have to do is keep an eye on your typically Tuscan-style roast. You can keep the Italian theme going with the drinks you serve.

ham and melon platter

TO DRINK Cinzano Bianco and soda (see p.23)—(its sweetness and delicate herbal notes will work perfectly.)

Tuscan-style roast veal and wild mushrooms

with roast new potatoes and buttered spinach

TO DRINK An elegant Chianti Classico Riserva.

grape and lemon mascarpone tart

TO DRINK A glass of gently sparkling honeysuckle sweet Moscato d'Asti, served well chilled in Champagne flutes.

ham and melon platter

For colour contrast you need an orange Canteloupe or Charentais melon and a green Galia, Ogen or Honeydew melon, and some thinly sliced Parma ham or prosciutto cotto all'erbe. Quarter and seed the melons, cut the wedges off the skin, then cut them into thick slices. Arrange on a big plate along with loosely draped slices of ham. The platter wants to look quite casual—lavish and generous, rather than arranged into perfectly lined up rows.

Serve the platter with some olive breadsticks and mini ciabattas, refreshed in the oven.

Italian aperitivos

Like the French, the Italians have a huge range of bittersweet aperitifs or aperitivos to get the tastebuds going including such drinks as Campari, Cinzano, and Aperol. Though less fashionable than they once were, they can be delicious with food and are refreshingly low in alcohol.

To make a Cinzano and soda (pictured left), put 4–5 ice cubes in a glass, fill half to two-thirds of the way up with Cinzano Bianco and top up with chilled soda water.

The charming Venetian sparkling wine Prosecco also makes a fine aperitivo. Mix it with freshly pressed peach juice for a classic Bellini cocktail.

Tuscan-style roast veal with wild mushrooms

I ate a dish like this at Castello di Brolio in Tuscany and couldn't wait till I got home to recreate it. It's a brilliant dish to match with wine—light but intensely flavorful—the perfect partner for a Chianti Classico Riserva.

2¼ lb. boned, rolled loin or rack of veal or pork (ask the butcher to give you the bones)
3 tablespoons olive oil
3 tablespoons butter
1 onion, cut into 8
1 large carrot, cut into chunks
3 large garlic cloves, peeled and quartered
3 sprigs of rosemary
1 cup dry Italian white wine
1 cup fresh chicken stock or light vegetable stock made with ½ organic bouillon cube
5 oz. wild mushrooms
2 teaspoons all-purpose flour
a few drops of Marsala or sweet sherry (optional)
sea salt and freshly ground black pepper

a large, deep, lidded and flameproof casserole

Serves 6

Preheat the oven to 400°F. Pat the veal dry and season all over with salt and pepper. Put the casserole over medium heat, add 1½ tablespoons of the olive oil, heat for a minute, then add 1 tablespoon of the butter. When the foaming dies down, put in the veal, bones, onion, and carrot and brown on all sides, turning regularly.

Add the garlic and rosemary to the casserole, stir and add 3 tablespoons of the white wine. Cover with a lid and transfer to the oven. Roast for about 2 hours. Check occasionally that the meat and vegetables aren't burning and add a little more white wine if necessary.

Remove the veal from the casserole and set aside on a warmed carving plate. Cover lightly with foil and let rest for at least half an hour.

Pour off any surface fat from the juices in the casserole, then add the remaining white wine and bring to a boil, working in the tasty caramelized juices stuck on the side of the casserole. Simmer and reduce the liquid by half, then add half the stock and simmer for another 10 minutes. Strain through a fine sieve.

Heat the remaining butter in a small skillet and fry the mushrooms until the butter and any liquid have almost evaporated. Stir in the flour. Pour in the strained stock, bring to a boil and simmer for 5 minutes. Add a little more stock if the sauce seems too thick. Check the seasoning, add salt and pepper to taste and a dash of Marsala if you like a touch of sweetness.

For a rack of veal, offer the sauce separately, otherwise finely slice the meat, arrange on a warmed platter and spoon over the sauce. Serve with roast new potatoes and buttered spinach (see right.)

roast new potatoes with olive oil

3 tablespoons olive oil
1½–2 lbs. baby new potatoes, washed and dried
sea salt and freshly ground black pepper

Serves 6

Preheat the oven to 400°F (if not already on for the meat.) Measure the oil into a shallow roasting pan, tip in the potatoes and shake the pan so that they get evenly covered with oil. Put the pan in the oven and roast for about 35–40 minutes until the potatoes are nicely browned, turning them halfway through. Season lightly with salt and pepper.

buttered spinach

3 lbs. loose spinach leaves
2 tablespoons extra virgin olive oil
2 tablespoons butter
sea salt and freshly ground black pepper
freshly grated nutmeg, to taste

Serves 6

Tip the leaves into a bowl of cold water and give them a good swirl. Discard any damaged leaves and remove the central tough rib from the larger leaves. Drain and pack into a large saucepan without any extra water. Put the pan over low heat, cover and leave for about 5 minutes. Turn the leaves over (the bottom leaves should have collapsed.) Re-cover and cook for another 3–4 minutes until all the leaves have collapsed but are still bright green. Drain thoroughly in a colander pressing out the excess water. Return the leaves to the pan and chop roughly. Add the oil and butter and heat until the spinach is hot and the butter melted. Season to taste with salt, pepper, and nutmeg.

grape and lemon mascarpone tart

This is a really simple dessert that you can make with ready-made pastry dough. A gorgeous Italian lemon liqueur gives a sharp edge to the creamy mascarpone.

8 oz. ready-made puff pastry dough, thawed if frozen

2 large eggs, separated

2 tablespoons superfine sugar, plus 1 teaspoon for sprinkling

8 oz. mascarpone cheese

2½ tablespoons Limoncello (lemon liqueur)

8 oz. white seedless or halved and seeded grapes, rinsed and dried

8 oz. red seedless or halved and seeded grapes, rinsed and dried

1 teaspoon confectioners' sugar

a large, square or rectangular baking sheet, lightly greased

Serves 6–8

Preheat the oven to 400°F. Take the pastry out of the fridge and let it rest for 20 minutes. Roll out thinly and lift carefully onto the baking sheet. Use a sharp knife to trim around the edge to make an 11-inch round.

Lightly whisk the egg whites and brush a thin layer onto the pastry. Sprinkle with 1 teaspoon superfine sugar, then use a fork to prick the pastry all over. Bake for 10–12 minutes until puffy and brown. Let cool while you make the topping.

Tip the mascarpone cheese into a bowl and gradually work in the Limoncello. Using an electric hand-held whisk, beat the egg yolks with the remaining superfine sugar until pale, thick, and creamy. Gently fold the mascarpone mixture into the eggs until blended.

Transfer the cooled pastry base to a large serving plate. Spread over the mascarpone mixture with a spatula, taking it almost up to the edges. Scatter the grapes on top.

Sift over the confectioners' sugar and serve straight away, or chill the tart for a couple of hours, then sprinkle with confectioners' sugar when ready to serve.

a Provençal-style lunch

menu for 6

If you want to entertain friends in summer, what could be more appealing than a light, flavorful Mediterranean lunch? Start with a cool, refreshing pastis or a glass of rosé and some typically Provençal olive-based nibbles, then serve some simply seared tuna— cooked on the grill if you feel like firing it up. Finally, a classic apricot tart with a twist, flavored with the gorgeous southern French dessert wine, Muscat de Beaumes-de-Venise. Simple and stylish.

anchovy and green olive dip with ciabatta toasts
mini pissaladières

TO DRINK Pastis or a chilled dry rosé. Dilute pastis (I like Henri Bardouin) about 1:5 with cool (not ice) water. Serve in small tumblers.

seared tuna with tomatoes, arugula, and gremolata

TO DRINK The rosé will also go with the tuna.

apricot tart with Muscat de Beaumes-de-Venise

TO DRINK Muscat de Beaumes-de-Venise.

anchovy and green olive dip

This is one of the easiest dips or spreads you can make.

3½-oz. jar anchovy fillets marinated in olive oil with garlic and herbs*

2 tablespoons pitted green olives

⅓ cup Provençal or Spanish olive oil

1 tablespoon red wine vinegar

2–3 tablespoons warm water

freshly ground black pepper

For the topping:

¼ cup pitted green olives

3 tablespoons chopped flatleaf parsley

ciabatta toasts (see right) to serve

a selection of crudités (radishes, carrot, and fennel strips), to serve

Serves 6

Tip the anchovies and their oil into a food processor with the olives and whizz until smooth. Gradually add the olive oil until you have a mayonnaise-type consistency. Add the red wine vinegar and sufficient warm water to make a spreadable consistency. Season with black pepper.

Chop the remaining olives and parsley together for the topping. Spread the anchovy paste thinly over the toasts and spoon over a little of the green olive topping. Serve on a platter decorated with radishes, carrot sticks, and fennel strips.

* If you can't find marinated anchovies, buy ordinary anchovies in olive oil and add 1 garlic clove and 1 tablespoon finely chopped parsley to the mixture.

Time-saving tip: You could also spread some of the toasts with store-bought tapénade (a purée of capers, black olives, anchovies, and olive oil.)

ciabatta toasts

It's worth making a large batch of these, as they keep well.

2 ready-to-bake ciabatta loaves

olive oil spray or 4–6 tablespoons light olive oil

2 baking sheets

Makes about 30–32 slices

Preheat the oven to 350°F. Cut the ciabatta on the slant into fairly thin slices. Spray both sides with olive oil or pour the olive oil on the baking sheets and dip the slices of ciabatta in it. Bake for 15 minutes, turning the slices halfway through. Repeat with any remaining ciabatta slices. Let cool, then store the toasts in an airtight container.

mini pissaladières

For the topping:

2 tablespoons olive oil

2 large sweet onions (about 1 lb. in total), thinly sliced

1 garlic clove, finely chopped

1 teaspoon finely chopped thyme or ½ teaspoon dried thyme

5 oz. small pitted marinated black olives

sea salt and freshly ground black pepper

a few small basil leaves, to garnish

For the pastry:

3½ oz. Quark or cream cheese

7 tablespoons butter, cut into cubes

1 cup all-purpose flour

1 teaspoon baking powder

a good pinch of salt

a 3-inch pastry cutter
2 x 12-cup shallow tartlet pans

Makes about 12–14

Heat the oil in a large flameproof casserole or saucepan. Tip in the onions, then cook over a medium heat until they have begun to collapse (about 10 minutes.) Stir in the garlic and thyme, turn the heat down a little and continue to cook for another 30–40 minutes until the onions are soft and golden and any liquid has evaporated, taking care that they don't catch and burn. Season with salt and pepper and set aside to cool.

While the onions are cooking, make the pastry. Tip the Quark into a food processor with the softened butter and process until smooth. Sift the flour with the baking powder and salt and add to the creamed cheese and butter in 2 batches, using the pulse to incorporate it. Once the mixture starts to form a ball, turn it out of the processor onto a floured board and form it into a flat disc. Put it in a plastic bag and chill for an hour in the fridge.

When ready to cook the tartlets, heat the oven to 425°F. Roll out the pastry quite thinly. Stamp rounds out of the pastry, re-rolling the trimmings as necessary, and lay them in the cups of the tartlet pans. Spoon in teaspoonfuls of the cooled onion mixture and top with an olive. Bake for 15–20 minutes until the pastry is puffed up and golden. Cool for 10 minutes, then remove the tarts carefully from the pan and arrange on a plate. Scatter with a few small basil leaves and serve. You can bake and freeze these, then reheat them from frozen in a moderate oven.

2 unwaxed lemons

3 large garlic cloves

a large handful of parsley

2 rounded tablespoons capers, rinsed if salted

6 fresh tuna steaks, about 5 oz. each

12 oz. pomodorino or other cherry tomatoes

3½ oz. arugula

sea salt and freshly ground black pepper

extra virgin olive oil, to drizzle

Serves 6

seared tuna with tomatoes, arugula, and gremolata

*This simple dish can equally well be adapted to a broiler or outdoor grill.**

First make the gremolata. Grate the zest finely from the lemons, taking care not to remove too much white pith. Peel the garlic cloves and chop them finely. Take the tough ends off the parsley stalks and finely chop the leaves. Roughly chop the capers, then pull all the ingredients together on the cutting board and chop them together to mix them thoroughly. Set aside in a bowl. Quarter the lemons.

When you're ready to cook, heat a ridged stovetop grill pan until almost smoking (about 3 minutes.) Rub both sides of the tuna steaks with olive oil and season with sea salt rubbed between your fingers and black pepper. Lay as many tuna steaks as you can fit in the grill pan and cook for about 1½–2 minutes, depending on the thickness and how rare you like them. Turn them over and cook the other side for 1–1½ minutes. Set aside on a warmed serving dish and cover lightly with foil. Repeat with the remaining tuna steaks. Rinse the pan under hot running water, dry with paper towels and reheat until very hot. Add 2 tablespoons oil and tip in the tomatoes. Cook for 1–1½ minutes, shaking the pan till the skins start to split then turn off the heat. To serve, put a small handful of arugula on each plate, top with a few tomatoes and lay the tuna steaks alongside. Drizzle the tuna and salad with olive oil and a good squeeze of lemon juice, and sprinkle over the gremolata. Serve with some authentic French crusty baguette or sourdough.

* If you use the broiler or outdoor grill to cook the tuna, just sauté the tomatoes quickly in a skillet to serve with the salad.

apricot tart with Muscat de Beaumes-de-Venise

This is my version of a brilliantly simple recipe from award-winning food writer Alastair Hendy. If you've never made a tart in your life, you could make this.

12 oz. ready-made puff pastry dough, thawed if frozen
1½ lbs. ripe apricots
2 tablespoons ground almonds
2 tablespoons superfine sugar
2 tablespoons Muscat de Beaumes-de-Venise
3 tablespoons soft-set apricot jam
Greek yogurt or vanilla ice cream, to serve

a shallow, rectangular, non-stick baking pan

Serves 6

Preheat the oven to 425°F and take the pastry out of the fridge about 20 minutes before you want to unroll it.

Halve and pit the apricots (you can cut the bigger ones into thirds.) Roll the pastry out thinly and lay it on the baking pan, trimming off any pastry that overhangs the edges. Prick the base with the prongs of a fork and shake over the ground almonds in an even layer. Sprinkle over 1 tablespoon of the sugar. Arrange the apricot halves or thirds in rows over the surface of the tart, leaving a narrow border around the edge and propping up each row on the one behind it. Spoon over the remaining sugar. Bake in the preheated oven for 30–35 minutes until the pastry is risen and the edges of the fruit are beginning to caramelize.

Spoon the jam into a small saucepan, add the Muscat and warm gently over low heat, stirring until smooth. Brush the warm glaze over the apricots and serve the tart with double cream or vanilla ice cream.

a summer picnic

menu for 6

Picnic food doesn't have to be rough and ready, as this sophisticated menu shows. Get ahead by making the Sun-dried Tomato, Olive, and Basil Bread, Lavender Shortbread, and Homemade Lemonade in advance, leaving you only the Chicken Tonnato Pasta Salad to assemble on the day (watch out—everyone is going to want the recipe!) Short of time? The menu is easy to adapt to a store-bought meal. Just buy a nice quiche, some ready-made shortbread, and some of the lovely traditional lemonades that are now available.

sun-dried tomato, olive, and basil bread with
handcut salami

chicken tonnato pasta salad

fresh peaches and cherries with lavender shortbread

homemade lemonade

TO DRINK Rosé is the perfect wine for this summery menu. I'd suggest a drier style from southern France or Spain (where it is called rosado), but if you prefer the fuller, fruitier New World style that is more like a light red, by all means go for it. The important thing is to keep it cold. Chill well beforehand and transport in insulated bags.

sun-dried tomato, olive, and basil bread

These easy breads are very popular in France where they somewhat confusingly call them "cake." They're like a cross between a savory bread and a quiche, and delicious to nibble with drinks.

1⅓ cups all-purpose flour

1 tablespoon baking powder

3 large eggs

6 tablespoons milk

6 tablespoons olive oil

3½ oz. mature Gruyère cheese, grated

3½ oz. sun-dried tomatoes in oil*, drained and roughly chopped

2 oz. pitted black olives marinated with herbs, roughly chopped

a small handful of basil leaves, roughly sliced

sea salt and freshly ground black pepper

a 12 x 4-inch rectangular, non-stick loaf pan, lightly greased and floured

Serves 6

Preheat the oven to 350°F. Sift the flour with the baking powder and season well with salt and black pepper. Whisk the eggs and whisk in the milk and oil. Tip two-thirds of the liquid into the flour, beat well, then add the remaining liquid. Mix in the Gruyère, tomatoes, olives, and basil, then tip into the prepared loaf pan. Bake in the preheated oven for 50 minutes or until a skewer comes out clean. Cool, then remove from the pan. Wrap in foil and keep in the fridge. Serve at room temperature, sliced and cut into halves or squares. You could also serve a plate of some chunky handcut, slices of salami that can be eaten with your fingers.

* If the sun-dried tomatoes come in oil, use a couple of tablespoons of the tomato-flavored oil to replace the olive oil in this recipe.

chicken tonnato pasta salad

This is a really easy yet impressive pasta salad. Don't be daunted by the rather long list of ingredients —the gremolata is based on pretty well the same ingredients as the sauce, but simply chopped rough for added texture.

2 cups fresh chicken stock or made with 1 organic bouillon cube

1 cup dry white wine

1 small onion, sliced

1 celery rib, trimmed and cut into 3 pieces

1 bay leaf

2 slices of unwaxed lemon

8–10 black peppercorns

4 skinless, boneless chicken breasts (about 1 lb. 5 oz. in total)

7 oz. dried egg pasta shapes

8 halved, grilled artichoke hearts (optional)

1 tablespoon roughly chopped flatleaf parsley

For the dressing:

3½ oz. premium (preferably Spanish) tuna, drained of oil

2 tablespoons small capers, rinsed

about 2 tablespoons freshly squeezed lemon juice

3 canned or jarred anchovy fillets, rinsed and finely chopped

1 cup mayonnaise

a pinch of cayenne pepper

For the gremolata:

5–6 canned or jarred anchovy fillets, rinsed and chopped

2 scallions, trimmed and thinly sliced

grated zest of 1 small unwaxed lemon or ½ large one

1 tablespoon small capers

3 tablespoons chopped flatleaf parsley

Also pack:

3 heads Boston lettuce, washed and crisped in the fridge, or a bag of mixed salad greens or arugula

1 lb. cherry tomatoes

a small bottle of olive oil

Serves 6

Pour the stock and wine into a large saucepan, big enough to take the chicken breasts in a single layer. Bring to a boil, add the onion, celery, bay leaf, lemon, and peppercorns and simmer for 5 minutes. Carefully lower the chicken breasts into the stock, adding some boiling water, if needed, to cover them. Bring back to a boil, then turn the heat right down and simmer very slowly for another 5 minutes. Turn the heat off, cover the pan, and let the chicken cool in the stock. This will take about 4–5 hours.

Once the chicken is cool, make the dressing. Put the drained tuna in a food processor with the capers, lemon juice, and anchovy fillets and whizz until you have a paste. Add the mayonnaise and cayenne pepper and whizz again until smooth. Turn into a large bowl. Put all the ingredients for the gremolata on a cutting board and chop them together.

Cook the pasta following the instructions on the package and refresh with ice water.

Remove the chicken from the poaching liquid and cut it into rough chunks. Add the chicken, pasta, and gremolata to the dressing and toss lightly. Check the seasoning, adding more lemon juice or cayenne pepper to taste if you think it needs it (you shouldn't need salt.) Transfer to a large plastic container, arrange the artichoke hearts, if using, over the top and sprinkle with parsley.

To assemble, arrange a handful of salad greens on each plate, scatter over a few tomatoes, drizzle over a little olive oil, then spoon the salad on top. Serve with some crusty bread.

homemade lemonade

You will need a juicer to make this absolutely delicious lemonade—in fact, it's almost worth buying one just to make it.

¾ cup superfine sugar
4 large juicy unwaxed lemons, plus 1 extra, sliced, to garnish
1¾ pints still or sparkling mineral water, chilled
a few sprigs of mint
plenty of ice, to serve

Makes 6–8 glasses

Put the sugar in a saucepan with ⅔ cup water. Heat over low heat, stirring until the sugar has completely dissolved, then bring to a boil and boil for 5 minutes without stirring. Take off the heat and leave to cool. Cut 2 of the lemons into small chunks and pass through the feeder tube of a juicer. They should produce about ⅔ cup thick juice. Squeeze the remaining lemons (again, that should yield about ⅔ cup) and add to the other juice. Stir in the sugar syrup you've made.

Chill the lemon concentrate until ready to use. Either pour into a large pitcher full of ice and pour in an equal amount of chilled still or sparkling mineral water, or pour a couple of shots of lemonade into a tumbler full of ice and top up with chilled mineral water. Garnish with lemon slices and sprigs of mint

Variation:

Raspberry lemonade

Purée (in a food processor or force through a nylon-mesh sieve) 1 cup of fresh or frozen raspberries and sweeten with 2 tablespoons sugar syrup (see recipe above.) Stir into the lemonade base and dilute as described. Decorate with lemon slices and a few whole raspberries.

lavender shortbread

Homemade shortbread is unbelievably easy to make. Cornstarch will make it smoother; ground rice or fine semolina more crumbly and rustic.

Preheat the oven to 300°C. Put the sugar and butter in a food processor and process until light and fluffy (or beat together with an electric hand-held whisk.) Add the lavender essence or flowers and whizz again. Add half the flour and pulse to incorporate, then add the remaining flour and pulse again. Add the cornstarch and pulse again until incorporated. (Or add in stages, by hand, beating with a wooden spoon then bring the mixture together with your hands.) Tip the mixture into a baking pan and spread out until even. Mark the shortbread with a sharp knife, dividing it into 18 squares, and prick lightly with the prongs of a fork. Bake in the preheated oven for about 40–45 minutes until pale gold in color. Sprinkle with the remaining sugar, put back in the oven and cook for another 5 minutes. Remove the pan from the oven, set aside for 10 minutes, then cut along the lines you've marked again. Remove the shortbread squares carefully with a palate knife and lay on a wire rack to finish cooling. Store in an airtight container.

¹/₃ cup superfine sugar, plus extra for sprinkling

1 stick plus 5 tablespoons butter, softened

¹/₄–¹/₂ teaspoon concentrated lavender essence or 1 tablespoon finely chopped dried lavender flowers

1¹/₃ cups all-purpose flour

¹/₂ cup cornstarch, ground rice or fine semolina

a 11 x 7 inch, shallow, rectangular baking pan

Makes 18 shortbreads

a seafood lunch

menu for 6

Even if you're not by the coast, it's great to host a seafood lunch, especially for health-conscious friends who like lighter food. Fish is such a popular option these days. Wine lovers will also appreciate the chance to share a special botle of white wine, that this simple elegant menu will show off quite perfectly. Then, having been virtuous, everyone will fall on the gorgeous creamy dessert, a lovely summer spin on the classic Italian tiramisù.

little seafood aspics with white wine and dill

TO DRINK A fine, minerally unoaked white such as Chablis, Sancerre, Pouilly Fumé, or a Spanish Albariño, that won't overwhelm the delicate flavors and texture of the aspics.

Sicilian-spiced sea bass with grilled tomatoes and baby fennel

TO DRINK Carry on drinking the same wine as with the first course or pick up on the Sicilian theme with a modern Sicilian white.

strawberry tiramisù

TO DRINK This will pair beautifully with a well-chilled glass of Moscato d'Asti or demi-sec sparkling wine.

little seafood aspics with white wine and dill

These delectable little aspics take a bit of time to assemble, but you can make them well ahead and they look really fabulous.

¾ cup light dry white wine, such as Frascati

1½ tablespoons Thai fish sauce

6 sheets of leaf gelatine (or enough to set 1 pint of liquid)

7 oz. fresh queen (small) scallops, halved

7 oz. cooked shelled shrimp, thawed if frozen

freshly squeezed juice of 1 lemon and 1 lime, strained

3 oz. smoked salmon, cut into thin strips

4–5 sprigs of dill, broken into smaller sprigs

white pepper

6 lowball glasses or glass dishes, chilled in the fridge

Serves 6

Pour the white wine into a saucepan, bring to a boil and reduce by half. Pour into a measuring pitcher, add the fish sauce, and any liquid from the shrimp, then top up with cold water up to the 1 pint mark. Lay the gelatine in a shallow dish and sprinkle over 3 tablespoons cold water. Pour the white wine mixture back into the saucepan and bring to a boil. Turn the heat right down, add the scallops and poach for 2 minutes. Remove the scallops with a slotted spoon and set aside to cool. Add the soaked gelatine to the poaching liquid and stir until thoroughly dissolved. Strain the mixture into a bowl, then place that bowl in a larger bowl of ice water to cool quickly.

Meanwhile, marinate the cooled scallops and shrimp in the lemon and lime juice with a little white pepper. Once the stock has cooled down, start assembling the aspics. Drain the shrimp and scallops from their marinade. Place a few shrimp, scallops, and pieces of smoked salmon in the bottom of each chilled glass, sprinkle over a couple of sprigs of dill then spoon over 2–3 tablespoons of the cooled stock. Place the glasses carefully in the fridge for the jelly to set (about 45 minutes), then repeat with the next layer and the next until all the seafood and dill is used up. Try and mix up the ingredients, so you get a multicolored effect and make sure the final layer is completely covered with stock. The aspics should be ready to eat within an hour or 2 of making them, but you can make them to eat the next day. Serve with fine crispbreads or thinly cut slices of light rye bread and unsalted butter.

Sicilian-spiced sea bass with grilled tomatoes and baby fennel

A simple dish that you can cook at the tableside if you're eating outdoors.

Soak the skewers in water for half an hour before you start. Heat a charcoal grill.

Crush the fennel seeds, oregano, cumin seeds, salt, peppercorns, and red pepper flakes together thoroughly in a mortar with a pestle. Make 3 slashes in each side of the fish with a sharp knife. Spray the fish with olive oil and rub the pounded spices over the fish and into the slits. Cut 2 of the lemons in half vertically, then cut 1½ into thin slices. Cut or tear the bay leaves into halves or thirds. Place half a slice of lemon and a piece of bay leaf in each slit. Cut each fennel bulb in quarters lengthways and thread the cherry tomatoes onto the skewers. Spray the fish, fennel, and tomatoes with oil and grill over medium heat until charred, turning them halfway through, removing them as they are cooked. Serve with wedges of lemon.

* If whole fish don't appeal, you could make this recipe with tuna or swordfish steaks.

Conventional cooking: You could cook the fish under a conventional broiler or, in the case of tuna or swordfish, in a nonstick skillet.

1 rounded teaspoon fennel seeds

1 rounded teaspoon dried oregano

1 teaspoon cumin seeds

1 teaspoon sea salt crystals

1 teaspoon green or black peppercorns

¼ teaspoon dried red pepper flakes

6 small sea bass, gutted and scaled (ask the fishmonger or assistant at the fish counter to do this for you)*

extra virgin olive oil spray

3 unwaxed lemons

a few bay leaves

4 baby fennel bulbs

12 oz. cherry tomatoes

wedges of lemon, to serve

6 wooden kabob skewers

Serves 6

strawberry tiramisù

This is a slight adaptation of a fantastic recipe from Italian cookery writer Valentina Harris, which I first tasted on one of her cooking courses in Tuscany.

1 pint fresh ripe strawberries

5 hard amaretti cookies

2 large eggs, separated

3 tablespoons superfine sugar

¼ teaspoon pure vanilla extract

4 tablespoons white rum

8 oz. mascarpone cheese, at room temperature

3 tablespoons whipping cream

6 tablespoons apple juice

3 oz. savoiardi (ladyfinger biscuits)

a medium–large, deep, glass dessert bowl

Serves 6

Hull the strawberries. Measure out ½ cup and chop them finely. Slice the remaining strawberries and set aside. Put the amaretti cookies in a plastic bag, seal, then hit them with a rolling pin until they are the consistency of coarse breadcrumbs.

Beat the egg yolks in a bowl with an electric hand-held whisk or a whisk until pale yellow and fluffy, gradually adding the sugar as you go. Add the vanilla extract and a tablespoon of the white rum. Tip the mascarpone cheese into a large bowl, beat with a wooden spoon to soften, then gradually add the egg yolk mixture and beat until smooth. In another bowl, whisk the egg whites until they just hold a soft peak. Fold the chopped strawberries into the mascarpone cheese mixture, then carefully fold in the egg whites.

Whip the whipping cream to a similar consistency then fold that in too, together with a third of the crushed amaretti cookies. Mix the remaining rum with the apple juice. Dip some of the savoiardi in the apple-rum mixture and lay across the base of your bowl. Reserving some sliced strawberries for decoration, arrange a layer of strawberries over the savoiardi, then cover with a layer of mascarpone cream. Repeat with 1 or 2 more layers of soaked savoiardi, strawberries, and mascarpone cream, finishing with the mascarpone cream. Cover the bowl tightly with plastic wrap and chill in the fridge for at least 5 hours.

About 1 hour before you serve up, sprinkle the remaining amaretti cookies over the top of the tiramisù, then decorate with the remaining strawberries. Return the tiramisù to the fridge until you are ready to serve it.

an around-the-world barbecue

menu for 8

Give your barbecue a glamorous globetrotting theme with this menu, that roams from South America to the eastern Mediterranean. I've suggested a couple of delicious pitcher drinks as an alternative to wine, as a touch of sweetness really helps with grilled flavors. To refresh your palate at the end of the meal, go for the delicious and pretty sparkling wine jellies.

gazpacho shots
pork and olive and cheese empanadas

TO DRINK A zesty Chilean Sauvignon Blanc or Spanish Rueda will pair well with both these dishes.

butterflied leg of lamb with cumin, lemon and garlic
kisir

TO DRINK A fruity, medium-bodied red such as a Merlot or Shiraz (you don't want too full-bodied a red with spicy or chargrilled foods.) Alternatively, serve one of the two pitcher drinks below.

sparkling Shiraz and summer berry jellies
sparkling peach and blueberry jellies

exotic Sea Breeze
watermelon and strawberry cooler

pork and olive empanadas

Empanadas are like mini-pasties—in fact they're believed to have been introduced to Mexico by the Cornish tin miners who came to work in the tin and silver mines.

3 tablespoons light olive oil

1 lb. ground pork

1 onion, finely chopped

1 garlic clove, finely chopped

2 tablespoons tomato concentrate

½ teaspoon apple pie spice

½ cup tomato purée or passata

1 tablespoon cider vinegar

10 large pitted green olives marinated in garlic and herbs, finely chopped

2 tablespoons finely chopped parsley

sea salt and freshly ground black pepper

1 lb. ready-made puff pastry dough, thawed if frozen

1 large egg, beaten

2 large baking sheets, greased
a 3½-inch cookie cutter

Serves 8

Heat 1 tablespoon of the olive oil in a large skillet and brown the mince. Remove to a bowl with a slotted spoon and pour off any remaining fat and meat juices. Add the remaining 2 tablespoons oil to the pan and fry the chopped onion for about 6–7 minutes until beginning to brown. Add the chopped garlic, fry for a few seconds, then return the meat to the pan. Add the tomato concentrate, stir in thoroughly and cook for a minute, then add the apple pie spice, tomato purée, and cider vinegar. Bring to a boil and simmer for 10–15 minutes until the liquid has been absorbed.

Stir in the chopped olives and parsley and season to taste with salt and pepper. Set aside until cool (about 1 hour.) Roll out the pastry on a floured board or counter. Cut out rounds with the cookie cutter and place a teaspoonful of the pork filling in the center of each one. Dampen the edges with water, fold over, and press the edges together. Repeat until you have used up all the pastry and filling, re-rolling the pastry trimmings as necessary. At this point you can refrigerate or freeze the empanadas until you are ready to cook them.

To cook, preheat the oven to 425°F. Cut a small slit in each empanada with a sharp knife. Brush with beaten egg and place on the baking sheets. Bake in the preheated oven for 8–10 minutes until puffed up and golden (slightly longer if cooking them from frozen.) Serve warm.

Time-saving tip: you could serve store-bought Mexican-style dips, such as Salsa Fresca and Guacamole.

cheese empanadas

1 garlic clove, roughly chopped

½ teaspoon salt

8 oz. cottage cheese

¼ teaspoon sweet (dulce) pimentón or paprika

2 heaping tablespoons finely chopped shallot

2 heaping tablespoons finely chopped parsley

salt and freshly ground black pepper

Serves 8

Put the garlic in a mortar with the salt and pound with a pestle until you have a paste. Tip into the cottage cheese along with the pimentón, shallot, and parsley and mix thoroughly. Season with salt and pepper. Take teaspoonfuls of the mixture and use to fill the empanadas, as described on the left.

gazpacho shots

This wonderfully refreshing summer soup makes a perfect appetizer. You could also serve it in small bowls with its usual garnish of finely chopped tomato, onion, cucumber, and red bell pepper and a few crispy croûtons if you prefer to eat it that way.

¼–½ mild Spanish onion, roughly chopped

1 red bell pepper, seeded and quartered

½ cucumber, peeled, seeded and chopped

1 lb. fresh tomatoes, peeled and chopped

14-oz.-can best-quality Italian tomatoes

1 garlic clove, crushed with ½ teaspoon salt or 1 teaspoon fresh garlic paste

3 tablespoons red wine vinegar

2 tablespoons extra virgin olive oil

a few sprigs of basil

salt, freshly ground black pepper, lemon juice, and hot pepper sauce, (such as Tabasco), to taste

cucumber batons and very finely diced red pepper, to garnish

Makes 16 shot glasses

Put the chopped onion in a food processor, together with three-quarters of the bell pepper, roughly chopped, and the cucumber and whizz until smooth. Add the fresh tomatoes, whizz again and then add the canned tomatoes, the garlic paste, vinegar and olive oil and whizz again. Transfer to a bowl, add the basil, and refrigerate for a couple of hours. Remove the basil and pass the soup through a fine-mesh nylon sieve, pressing it well to extract all the liquid. Return to the fridge until ready to serve. Add enough ice water to make a drinkable consistency, then check the seasoning, adding salt and pepper to taste, a little vinegar or a squeeze of lemon, and a dash of hot pepper sauce if you like. Serve in shot glasses with a sprinkle of tiny cubes of red bell pepper and a cucumber baton as a swizzle stick.

butterflied leg of lamb with cumin, lemon, and garlic

A butterflied leg of lamb—one where the bone is removed and the meat opened up to create a huge flat piece of meat—is one of the tastiest, simplest, and most impressive dishes to grill. Order it in advance from a butcher and he'll do all the hard work for you. Serve with kisir, a salad of mixed greens, and some flatbreads.

2 large garlic cloves, chopped

1 teaspoon coarse sea salt

1 tablespoon cumin seeds

1 teaspoon coriander seeds

1 teaspoon Herbes de Provence

1/2 teaspoon black peppercorns

1/4 teaspoon crushed chiles

freshly squeezed juice of 1 lemon

3 tablespoons olive oil

1 large butterflied leg of lamb (4 1/2–5 lbs.)

a large roasting pan

Serves 8

Put the garlic, salt, cumin seeds, coriander seeds, Herbes de Provence, black peppercorns, and chiles in a mortar and pound with a pestle until the garlic breaks down and you have a thick paste. Gradually work in the lemon juice and oil. Work over the meat with a small, sharp knife, cutting away any excess fat, then cut the meat into 2 or 3 manageable pieces. Put the meat in a roasting pan, rub in the marinade, cover, and leave in a cool place for 1–2 hours. Heat an outdoor grill to the maximum setting and cook the meat for 15–20 minutes, depending on the thickness of the meat and your preference, turning it halfway through the cooking time. Remove to a warmed carving plate, cover with foil and let rest for 15 minutes before slicing thinly.

kisir

This Turkish recipe is the perfect party salad. You can vary it depending on what you have available, substituting walnuts for hazelnuts or pistachios, for example, adding some olives or some finely snipped dried apricots or replacing the dill with fresh cilantro.

1 1/2 cups bulgur wheat

1/4 cup roasted hazelnuts, chopped

1/4 cup pistachio nuts, chopped

5–6 scallions, trimmed and thinly sliced

1/2 cucumber, peeled, seeded and finely chopped

1 red bell pepper, halved, seeded and finely chopped

3 ripe tomatoes, peeled and finely chopped

1 pomegranate

freshly squeezed juice of 2 lemons

1/2 teaspoon salt

1 teaspoon ground cumin

1 teaspoon red pepper flakes

3 tablespoons extra virgin olive oil

1 tablespoon pomegranate syrup or 2 teaspoons balsamic vinegar with 1 teaspoon sugar

5 tablespoons finely chopped parsley

3 tablespoons finely chopped mint leaves

3 tablespoon finely chopped dill

sea salt and freshly ground black pepper

Serves 8

Put the bulgur wheat in a large heatproof bowl and pour over enough boiling water to just cover the grain. Leave for 15 minutes for the liquid to absorb, then pour over plenty of cold water, swirl the grain around and tip into a sieve. Squeeze the grain with your hands to extract any excess water and return the grain to the bowl.

Add the nuts, scallions, cucumber, bell pepper, and tomatoes (including the seeds and pulp). Halve the pomegranate and scoop out the seeds, reserving the juice and discarding the pith. Add the pomegranate seeds to the salad.

Whisk the lemon juice and reserved pomegranate juice with the salt, cumin, and red pepper flakes, whisk in the olive oil and pomegranate syrup and season with salt and pepper. Tip into the salad and mix well.

Finally, mix in the chopped herbs. Toss well together and check the seasoning, adding more salt, pepper, or lemon juice to taste. Cover and set aside for at least an hour before serving for the flavours to infuse.

Beers for a barbecue:

Ice-cold lager is the standard fare for barbecues, but a blonde ale or amber lager makes much more rewarding drinking.

sparkling Shiraz and summer berry jellies

9 sheets of gelatine (or enough to set 1¼ pints of liquid)

1 bottle (1¼ pints) sparkling Shiraz or other sparkling red wine

1 lb. 5 oz. mixed fresh red berries, such as strawberries, raspberries, blackberries, blueberries, or redcurrants

2–3 tablespoons superfine sugar, depending on how ripe your berries are

6–8 tablespoons homemade sugar syrup* or store-bought gomme

8 shortball glasses or small glass serving dishes

Serves 8

Put the gelatine in a flat dish and sprinkle over 4 tablespoons cold water. Leave to soak for 3 minutes until soft. Heat the wine in a microwave or saucepan until hot but not at a boil. Tip the gelatine into the wine and stir to dissolve, then set aside to cool. Rinse the berries, cut the strawberries into halves or quarters, then put them in a shallow bowl, sprinkle over the sugar and leave them to macerate. Check the liquid jelly for sweetness, adding sugar syrup to taste.

Put an assortment of berries in the glasses, then pour over enough jelly to cover them. Put in the fridge to chill. As soon as the jelly has set (about 1 hour) add the rest of the fruit and jelly. Return the jellies to the fridge to set for another 45 minutes–1 hour before serving.

* To make the sugar syrup dissolve ½ cup granulated sugar in ½ cup water. Heat gently together in a pan. When all the grains are dissolved, bring to a boil and simmer for 2–3 minutes. Use it immediately or cool and store it for up to two weeks in the fridge.

sparkling nectarine and blueberry jellies

9 sheets of gelatine (or enough to set 1¼ pints of liquid)

1 bottle (1¼ pints) sparkling peach-flavored wine

3 ripe nectarines

2 tablespoons freshly squeezed lemon juice

7 oz. fresh blueberries, rinsed

8 shortball glasses or small glass serving dishes

Serves 8–10

Put the gelatine in a flat dish and sprinkle over 4 tablespoons cold water. Leave to soak for 3 minutes until soft. Heat the wine in a microwave or saucepan until hot but not at a boil. Tip the gelatine into the wine and stir to dissolve, then set aside to cool. Cut the nectarines into cubes and sprinkle with the lemon juice. Put a few blueberries and cubes of nectarine in the bottom of each glass then pour over jelly to cover. Put in the fridge to chill. As soon as the jelly has set, add the remaining fruit and jelly. Return to the fridge to set for another 45 minutes–1 hour before serving.

exotic Sea Breeze

A variation on the classic cocktail.

7 fl oz. vodka
14 fl oz. pomegranate juice
½ pint ruby grapefruit juice
3½ oz. freshly squeezed lime juice (from 2–3 limes)
2–3 teaspoons pomegranate syrup
1 pomegranate, halved and sliced
a few sprigs of fresh mint
ice cubes, to serve

Makes 6–8 glasses

Pour the vodka, pomegranate juice, ruby grapefruit juice, and lime juice into a large pitcher full of ice. Sweeten to taste with pomegranate syrup. Garnish with pomegranate seeds and sprigs of mint to serve.

watermelon and strawberry cooler

You can't really make this unless you have a juicer, but otherwise it's one of the easiest and most refreshing summer drinks.

1 large watermelon
1 lb. fresh strawberries, hulled, plus extra to garnish
1 unwaxed lemon, peeled and chopped
3½ fl oz. vodka (optional)
3 sprigs of mint, leaves roughly torn
ice cubes, to serve

Makes 6–8 glasses

Cut the watermelon in half, then cut off a thin slice for garnishing. Scoop out the pulp and cut into rough chunks. Feed the watermelon, strawberries, and lemon chunks through the juicer alternately. Put ice cubes into a pitcher (plus the vodka, if using.) Pour over the juice. Add the mint and stir well. Pour into glasses and decorate with a wedge of watermelon and a few slices of strawberry to serve.

a family Sunday lunch

menu for 6

When several generations are involved, it's always better to play it safe with the menu and stick to tried and trusted favorites like roast chicken and fruit desserts that even small children will enjoy. And not to make the menu too long or complicated—just two courses in this case. The good news though is that these simple dishes are a great foil for fine wines—which gives the adults a treat!

homemade cheese nibbles

Parmesan and pistachio biscuits

Cheddar crispies

TO DRINK There's a fantastic affinity between warm cheesy biscuits and Champagne or Champagne-style sparkling wines, so that would be a great way to kick off this meal.

superlative roast chicken with sausage meatballs

crunchy roast potatoes and buttery peas

TO DRINK Drink any light- or medium-bodied red wine—a red Burgundy or other Pinot Noir or a Merlot-based red such as St. Emilion would be my top choices.

raspberry, apple, and almond crumble

TO DRINK Serve a light, lemony Sauternes, or Sauternes-style dessert wine such as Monbazillac or Saussignac or a late-harvest Sauvignon or Semillon.

homemade cheese nibbles

It's easy enough to buy in crackers to have with a pre-lunch drink, but it's so simple to make your own. It can also be a fun thing to do with any budding young cooks in the family. These can be made ahead and then reheated.

Parmesan and pistachio biscuits

¾ cup all-purpose flour

3½ tablespoons butter, softened

½ cup finely grated mature Parmesan cheese, plus extra for topping

3 tablespoons finely chopped pistachio nuts

1 large egg yolk

½ teaspoon fine sea salt

cayenne pepper, to taste

a 2-inch cookie cutter
a baking sheet, lightly greased

Makes about 18–20 biscuits

Preheat the oven to 375°F. Put the flour, butter, Parmesan, nuts, and seasoning in a food processor and pulse until you have a crumbly mixture. Add the egg yolk and enough water (a teaspoon or two) to form a stiff dough. Transfer the dough to a lightly floured counter or board, knead lightly and roll out quite thinly. Stamp out rounds with the cookie cutter and carefully transfer them with a palate knife to the baking sheet. Re-roll the trimmings and stamp as many more biscuits as you can get out of the dough. Sprinkle the biscuits lightly with Parmesan and bake in the preheated oven for about 15–20 minutes, until lightly browned. Leave on the baking sheet for a few minutes then transfer to a wire rack to cool for 10–15 minutes. If not eating straight away, store in an airtight container then reheat at 325°F for 7–8 minutes before serving.

cheddar crispies

¾ cup plus 2 tablespoons all-purpose flour
½ teaspoon salt
1 stick butter, chilled and cut into small cubes
1 cup grated sharp cheddar cheese
½ cup crisped rice cereal
sesame seeds and poppy seeds, to garnish
freshly ground black pepper

2 baking sheets, lightly greased

Makes about 20 crispies

Preheat the oven to 350°F. Put the flour and salt in a bowl and season with pepper. Add the cubed butter and rub in until the mixture resembles coarse breadcrumbs. Add the grated cheese and crisped rice and pull the mixture together. Take spoonfuls of the mixture and roll them into small, walnut-sized balls. Arrange on the baking sheets and flatten each ball lightly with the prongs of a fork. Sprinkle half the crispies with sesame seeds and half with poppy seeds and bake for 15–20 minutes until lightly browned. Leave on the baking sheets for a few minutes, then transfer to a wire rack to cool for 10–15 minutes.

If not eating straight away, store in an airtight container, then reheat at 325°F for 7–8 minutes before serving.

superlative roast chicken with sausage meatballs

Everyone has their own favorite roast chicken recipe, but this is the one I go back to most often. I like to cook two small birds rather than one big one so that everyone has a chance to have their favorite bit. You can make a more sophisticated unthickened wine-based gravy if you prefer, but this is the type of gravy children (and grandparents) tend to go for!

2 small–medium chickens (about 3 lbs.), preferably organic
1 large unwaxed lemon
2 garlic cloves, unpeeled and flattened
2 small handfuls of parsley
1 tablespoon olive oil
2 tablespoons butter
sea salt and freshly ground black pepper

For the meatballs:
1 lb. best-quality traditional pork sausages
2 tablespoons finely chopped parsley
a little all-purpose flour for rolling

For the gravy:
2 tablespoons all-purpose flour
1²/₃ cup fresh chicken stock or made from 1 organic bouillon cube

a large roasting pan

Serves 6

Preheat the oven to 400°F. Grate a little zest from the lemon and reserve it for the sausage meatballs. Remove any giblets from inside the birds and stuff each of them with half a lemon, a flattened garlic clove, and a small handful of parsley. Heat the olive oil gently in a small saucepan, add the butter, then when it has melted brush the chickens with the oil and butter mixture. Season the birds with salt and pepper and place them in the roasting pan, breast-side upwards. Put in the preheated oven to roast for 20 minutes until the breast begins to brown. Turn the chickens on one side and roast for a further 15 minutes, while you make the sausage meatballs (these will be added to the pan and cooked with the chicken).

Slit the skins of the sausages and tip the meat into a bowl. Add the chopped parsley, lemon zest, and pepper and mix well. Form into about 18 small walnut-sized balls and brown lightly on all sides in a skillet. Carefully pour or spoon out most of the fat and juices that have accumulated in the roasting pan and reserve them. Turn the chickens onto their other side. Add the lightly browned meatballs and cook for another 15 minutes. Finally, turn the chickens breast-side

upwards again, turn the meatballs, baste the chickens with the remaining pan juices and cook for a final 10–15 minutes until the chickens are crisp and brown and fully cooked. Take the chickens and meatballs out of the oven and transfer to a warmed serving plate. Lightly cover with foil.

To make the gravy, skim the fat off the reserved juices. Pour off all except 3 tablespoons of fat from the pan, stir in the flour and cook for a minute. Add the skimmed juices and a third of the stock and bring to a boil, stirring and scraping off any dark sticky bits from the side of the pan. Add the remaining stock, then simmer until thick (about 3–4 minutes). Check the seasoning, adding salt and pepper to taste, and strain the gravy into a warmed pitcher.

Carve the chicken and serve with the meatballs, roast potatoes, and buttery peas or other child-friendly vegetables.

crunchy roast potatoes

3¹/₂ lbs. roasting potatoes
5–6 tablespoons rapeseed or vegetable oil
sea salt

a medium roasting pan

Serves 6

Preheat the oven to 400°F. Peel the potatoes, halve or quarter them depending how big they are and place them in a large saucepan. Cover with cold water and bring to a boil. Add a little salt, boil for 5 minutes, then drain the potatoes. Pour the oil into a roasting pan and tip in the potatoes, turning them in the oil. Roast the potatoes in the preheated oven for 45 minutes, turning them halfway through the cooking time. Turn the heat up to 425°F and continue to cook until the potatoes are crisp (about another 15–20 minutes.)

buttery peas

3 cups shelled fresh or frozen peas
a sprig of mint
2¹/₂ tablespoons butter, softened
2 tablespoons finely chopped parsley or snipped chives (optional)

Serves 6

Put the peas in a saucepan, add the mint, and cover with boiling water. Bring back to a boil and cook for about 3–5 minutes until the peas are tender. Drain, add the butter and herbs, if using, and toss together well. Serve immediately.

raspberry, apple, and almond crumble

The addition of raspberries to this otherwise traditional English crumble not only gives it a gorgeous color but creates a pleasing tartness that makes it a brilliant match with a fine dessert wine.

3 large tart apples, (such as Northern Spy), peeled, cored, and sliced

3–4 tablespoons superfine or granulated sugar

9 oz. fresh or frozen raspberries

For the topping:

1 cup plus 2 tablespoons all-purpose flour

1 oz. ground almonds

1 stick butter, chilled and cut into cubes

¼ cup superfine or granulated sugar

1 oz. flaked almonds (optional)

vanilla ice cream and/or half-and-half, to serve

a shallow ovenproof dish, lightly greased

Serves 6

Put the apples in a large saucepan. Sprinkle over 3 tablespoons sugar and add 3 tablespoons water. Cover the pan, place over low heat and cook for about 15 minutes, shaking the pan occasionally until the apple pieces are soft but still holding their shape. Stir in the raspberries and check for sweetness, adding a little extra sugar if it seems too sharp. Transfer to the prepared dish and let cool.

To make the topping, put the flour and ground almonds in a large bowl. Keep cutting the butter cubes into the flour mixture until you can't get the pieces of butter any smaller, then rub the butter and flour mixture together with your fingertips, until the mixture resembles coarse breadcrumbs. Stir in the sugar and carry on rubbing for another minute. Stir in the flaked almonds, if using.

When the fruit has cooled, set the oven to 400°F. Spread the crumble mixture evenly over the cooled fruit, making sure you cover the whole surface, then bake for about 35–40 minutes until the topping is golden and the fruit juices bubbling around the sides of the dish. Let cool for 10–15 minutes before serving.

a summer berry tea

menu for 12

A gorgeous, girly summer tea that's perfect for a celebration: a birthday, a christening, or just a special treat for mom. There are plenty of homemade treats if you have the time to bake or you could just make a couple of the recipes, like the meringues and the cupcakes, and buy the rest. Makes you wonder why we don't have tea more often...

&

mini choux puffs with crab and cilantro

strawberry and mascarpone tartlets

rose petal cupcakes

pink cava and strawberry jellies

raspberry and brown sugar meringues

old-fashioned white wine cup

TO DRINK There are plenty of delicious drinks to serve if you want to stick to pink—rosé Champagne (or sparkling Zinfandel if you want a wine with a touch more sweetness) and pink lemonade would be two good choices. Or Kir Royales made with a splash of raspberry-flavored liqueur and topped up with chilled sparkling wine.

mini choux puffs with crab and cilantro

3 tablespoons butter, cut into cubes

½ cup all-purpose flour, sifted with ¼ teaspoon fine sea salt

2 eggs, lightly beaten

8 oz. crabmeat

2 heaping tablespoons finely chopped fresh cilantro

2 heaping tablespoons mayonnaise

2 teaspoons finely chopped pickled ginger

1 tablespoon freshly squeezed lemon juice

a little grated lemon zest

sea salt and freshly ground black pepper

2 large baking sheets, lightly greased

Makes 24 puffs

Preheat the oven to 425°F. To make the choux puffs, melt the butter in ⅔ cup water in a saucepan and bring to a boil. Take off the heat, add the flour all at once, and beat with a wooden spoon until the dough comes away from the side of the pan. Let cool for 5 minutes, then gradually beat in the eggs until you have a stiff, glossy mixture. Rinse the baking sheets with cold water, shaking off any excess so they are slightly damp (this helps the pastry rise.) Using 2 teaspoons spoon small blobs of the mixture onto the sheets, then place in the preheated oven and cook for about 18–20 minutes until brown and well risen. Remove from the oven and cut a small slit in the base of each puff so that they don't collapse. Let cool on a wire rack.

Meanwhile, place the crabmeat in a bowl, taking care that you don't include any pieces of shell. Add the other ingredients and mix together lightly (you don't want to pound it into a paste.) Check the seasoning adding extra lemon juice or lemon zest and salt and pepper to taste.

When the choux puffs are cold, cut them in half with a serrated knife and fill with the crab mixture. Serve immediately.

strawberry and mascarpone tartlets

1¾ cups all-purpose flour

3 tablespoons confectioners' sugar

1 stick plus 5 tablespoons butter, chilled and cut into cubes

1 large egg yolk

a pinch of salt

8 oz. mascarpone cheese

2 tablespoons superfine sugar

½ teaspoon pure vanilla extract

1–2 tablespoons whipping cream

1 pint fresh strawberries, hulled and cut into 3

2 heaping tablespoons redcurrant jelly

a 3-inch pastry cutter
2 x 12-cup shallow tartlet pans

Makes 24 tartlets

To make the pastry, sift the flour and confectioners' sugar into a bowl. Cut the butter into the flour, then rub lightly between your fingertips until the mixture resembles coarse breadcrumbs. Mix the egg yolk with 3 tablespoons ice water, add to the bowl, mix lightly, and pull together into a ball, adding extra water if needed. Shape into a flat disc, put it in a plastic bag and refrigerate for at least half an hour. Roll out the pastry quite thinly and stamp out rounds, re-rolling the cuttings. Gently press the rounds into the cups in the tartlet pans. Prick the bases and chill for another half an hour. Preheat the oven to 375°F. Bake the pastry cases for about 15–20 minutes until lightly colored, then set aside and cool. Tip the mascarpone into a mixing bowl, add the sugar, vanilla extract, and a tablespoon of cream and beat until smooth. Add enough extra cream to give a firm but spoonable consistency. Put a heaping teaspoonful of mixture into each pastry case and top with 3 strawberry pieces, arranging them so that the pointed ends meet at the top. Melt the redcurrant jelly and brush it over the strawberries. You can chill the tarts briefly, but serve within 2 hours of making.

rose petal cupcakes

2 sticks butter, softened

1¼ cup superfine or granulated sugar

4 large eggs, beaten with 1½ teaspoons pure vanilla extract

2 cups self-rising flour, sifted twice

½ cup whole milk

For the frosting:

3 tablespoons butter, softened

a few drops of red food coloring

1½ cups confectioners' sugar, sifted twice

¼ teaspoon rosewater

a small pinch of salt

2–3 tablespoons whole milk

sugar roses or other cake decorations

2 x 12-cup muffin or cake pans
approximately 24 paper cakes cases

Makes 24 cakes

Preheat the oven to 350°F. Tip the butter into a large bowl and beat with an electric hand-held whisk until smooth. Add the sugar about a third at a time and continue to beat until pale yellow and fluffy. Gradually add the beaten eggs and vanilla extract, adding a spoonful of flour with the last few additions. Fold in the remaining flour alternately with the milk, taking care not to overmix. Spoon into the paper cases and bake for about 20–25 minutes until well risen and firm to the touch. Remove the pans from the oven for 5 minutes then transfer the cakes to a wire rack to cool.

To make the frosting, beat the butter until soft. Pour a few drops of red food coloring onto a teaspoon (easier to control than pouring straight from the bottle), then carefully add to the butter, pouring back any excess into the bottle. Gradually add the confectioners' sugar 2–3 tablespoonfuls at a time. Add the rosewater, salt, and enough milk to make a spreadable consistency. Spread on the tops of the cupcakes and decorate with the sugar roses. Leave for 2 hours before serving.

pink cava and strawberry jellies

12 sheets of gelatine (or enough to set 5 cups of liquid)

5 cups Cava Rosado or other sparkling rosé

2 pints fresh strawberries

2–3 tablespoons granulated sugar, depending on how ripe your strawberries are

⅓–½ cup homemade sugar syrup (see page 48) or shop-bought gomme

whipped cream or vanilla ice cream, to serve

12 wine glasses or small glass serving dishes

Serves 12

Lay the gelatine in a large flat dish and sprinkle over 5–6 tablespoons cold water. Leave to soak for 3 minutes until soft. Heat the wine in a microwave or saucepan until hot but not at a boil. Tip the soaked gelatine into the wine and stir to dissolve, then set aside to cool.

Rinse the strawberries, cut them into halves or quarters to give even-sized pieces and put them into a shallow bowl, sprinkle over the sugar, and leave them to macerate. Check the liquid jelly for sweetness, adding the sugar syrup to taste. Divide half the strawberries between the glasses then pour over enough jelly to cover them. Put in the fridge to chill. As soon as the jelly has set (about an hour,) add the rest of the fruit and jelly. Return to the fridge to set for another 45 minutes–1 hour before serving with whipped cream or ice cream.

* Adding a dash of strawberry-flavored syrup or liqueur to the liquid jelly will make this even more delicious.

raspberry and brown sugar meringues

I love the little explosions of fruit in the middle of these meringues. They won't keep as long as conventional meringues, so do eat them within two to three hours of making them.

4 large egg whites, at room temperature

¼ cup superfine sugar

¼ cup light brown sugar

1½ cups frozen raspberries, unthawed

2 large, non-stick baking sheets, lightly greased with flavorless oil, or lined with baking parchment

Makes 16 meringues

Preheat the oven to 300°F. Put the egg whites in a large, clean grease-free bowl and start to whisk them (easiest with an electric hand-held whisk.) Increase the speed as they begin to froth up, moving the whisk around the bowl, until they just hold a peak (about 2–3 minutes.) Gradually add the superfine sugar a teaspoonful at a time, beating the meringue well between each addition. When half the superfine sugar has been incorporated, add the rest of it a spoonful at a time. Gradually add the soft brown sugar, then gently fold in the frozen raspberries, ensuring that they are fully coated by the meringue.

Using 2 dessertspoons, carefully spoon the meringues onto the prepared baking sheets. Place in the preheated oven and immediately reduce the heat to 275°F. Bake for 1¼ hours until the meringues are firm. Turn off the heat and let the meringues cool in the oven.

You can refrigerate the meringues for up to 3 hours, lightly covered with plastic wrap, before serving.

old-fashioned white wine cup

The great virtue of white wine cups is that you can use a really basic, inexpensive dry white wine as the base. In fact, it's a positive advantage to do so. Most modern whites have too much up-front fruit flavor and alcohol for this delicate, quintessentially English summery drink.

1½ pints very dry white wine, such as basic Vin Blanc or Muscadet

1½ pints soda water, chilled

⅓ to ½ cup homemade sugar syrup (see page 48) or shop-bought gomme

3–6 tablesppons brandy

about 20 ice cubes, to serve

orange, lemon, apple, kiwi, strawberry, and cucumber slices, to serve

a few mint leaves, to garnish

Makes 16 glasses

Mix the wine and soda in a pitcher and add sugar syrup and brandy to taste. Prepare the fruit and add to the mix, together with ice cubes, just before serving. Serve in wine glasses, garnished with the mint leaves.

tea

A tea party is the perfect opportunity to serve some interesting teas and tisanes: Earl Grey or Lady Grey, for example, or fragrant Orange Pekoe. Ideally, you should make them from loose leaves in a teapot, warming the pot first and infusing them for 2–3 minutes. Encourage your guests to drink them without milk and with honey rather than sugar. Another delicious option is a tisane or infusion of fresh lemon verbena leaves (*verveine* to the French who are mad about it), which makes a really refreshing, slightly citrussy drink.

come over for a drink

great ideas for simple entertaining

The easiest way to entertain people is to invite them over for a drink. Of course, you don't just mean a drink, but a bite to eat too. In the past that might have meant a few nuts or chips, olives and cubes of cheese, or possibly a dip with a few crisp vegetables or crackers to dunk in it. Not a big deal because the presumption would have been that there was a "proper" meal to follow. Nowadays with both eating and entertaining being more relaxed and casual, it's more than likely that the food you serve will constitute a light meal, replacing dinner, and need to be more substantial.

Inviting friends over for a drink is more a message to your guests that this is a low-key affair without formal courses, that neither they or you has to make a special effort, and that you just want the pleasure of enjoying an evening with them. It's a good way to entertain when all parties are pressed for time, not least because these days, whatever food or drink you choose to serve, you can buy virtually everything. Whether it's Spanish tapas, Middle Eastern, or Mexican dips, Indian street snacks, or Japanese sushi, you can find it ready-made in a good store. All you have to do is present it with a little care and style, and choose an interesting drink to accompany it.

Over the next few pages you'll find some easy ideas for theming an invitation to drinks, which you can easily adapt to larger numbers. You'll also find some ideas in other sections of the book, such as the Provençal snacks on pages 28–29, and the Chinese dim sum on pages 122–123.

sushi and sake

Serve an attractive selection of ready-made sushi with chilled sake—you could lay on a few light beers or sparkling wine for those who don't think they like sake. If you want something sweet, you could serve some little jellies or Japanese-style cakes (which you can find in Asian stores or order them from a local Japanese restaurant.)

Indian street snacks

Serve a selection of ready-made classic deep-fried snacks, such as onion bhajias, pakoras, and samosas with fresh coriander chutney or raita and a choice of lighter beers (pale ales, pilseners, and wheat beers would make a good selection.) By all means lay on some wine—oddly, sparkling white wine works well with spicy snacks or an off-dry white such as Riesling. You could also serve jugs of mango lassi (yogurt mixed with mango purée and water.)

go Greek

Serve a selection of shop-bought mezedes such as hoummus, taramasalata, stuffed vine leaves, feta cheese, and marinated olives with warmed pita bread, and one of Greece's vivid lemony white wines, such as Assyrtiko from the island of Santorini. More adventurous guests might enjoy octopus or squid with ouzo. Finish with fresh fruits or syrup-drenched pastries served with the glorious Samos Muscat dessert wine.

beer and cheese

An alternative to wine and cheese that gives you a chance to explore and enjoy some of the fantastic craft beers that are now available. Choose four to six different styles and have a tasting, followed by some good artisanal cheeses and breads. You could even serve a cheesecake with a fruit beer to finish.

Margaritas and tostaditas

Why not have a get-together with a Mexican flavor? You can serve your Margaritas Mexican-style with tortilla chips and a simple salsa but here's a slightly dressier way of serving them.

shrimp and guacamole topping

For the marinade:
freshly squeezed juice of ½ a lime
1½ tablespoons olive oil
1 garlic clove, crushed
1 tablespoon finely chopped fresh cilantro

7 oz. peeled, cooked large shrimp
1 cup homemade or store-bought guacamole
large tortilla chips, to serve

Makes sufficient to top 12–14 large tortilla chips

Mix the ingredients for the marinade together and pour over the shrimp. Cover and marinate for at least an hour. Spoon the guacamole onto tortilla chips and top with marinated shrimp.

crab, mango, and basil topping

2 heaping tablespoons mayonnaise
1 small red chile, seeded and finely chopped
2 scallions, trimmed and finely chopped
a little finely grated fresh ginger (about ½ teaspoon)
1–2 tablespoons freshly squeezed lemon juice
6 oz. crabmeat
½ cup peeled and finely diced ripe mango, plus mango shavings made using a vegetable peeler or sharp knife, to garnish
6 large basil leaves
sea salt and cayenne pepper
large tortilla chips, to serve

Makes sufficient to top 12–14 large tortilla chips

Mix the mayonnaise with the chile, scallions, ginger, and 1 tablespoon of the lemon juice. Fold in the crab and mango. Season to taste with salt, cayenne pepper, and extra lemon juice. Refrigerate. Just before serving, finely shred the basil leaves and fold into the crab mixture. Spoon onto tortilla chips and top with a mango shaving.

classic frozen Margarita

24 ice cubes
freshly squeezed juice of 3–4 limes (about ⅔ cup)
1½ teaspoons superfine sugar
½ pint silver tequila
¼ pint Triple Sec, Cointreau, or Grand Marnier
1 lime, to garnish
salt (optional)*

8 wide-rimmed Martini or Margarita glasses, rims salted (optional)

Makes 6–8 drinks

Place the ice cubes in a blender with the lime juice and sugar. Whizz until it forms a frozen slush. Add the tequila and Triple Sec and whizz again. Pour into the prepared glasses and decorate with a slice of lime.

* The traditional presentation is to frost your glasses with salt. Simply run a wedge of lime round the rim and invert the glass in a saucer of sea salt.

iced strawberry Margaritas

1 pint fresh strawberries
4–6 tablespoons Cointreau or Triple Sec
1 pint store-bought strawberry sorbet
8 fl oz. silver tequila
2–4 tablespoons freshly squeezed lime juice
crushed ice, to serve

3–4 wide-rimmed Martini or Margarita glasses

Makes 3–4 drinks

Hull the strawberries and reserve a few for the garnish. Slice the rest roughly, then put half in a blender with 2 tablespoons Cointreau and whizz until smooth. Tip in half the sorbet, add half the tequila, and 1 tablespoon of the lime juice and whizz again. Taste, adjusting the amount of Cointreau or lime juice (or tequila!) if you think it needs it. Fill the glasses with crushed ice and put a few slices of the reserved strawberries in each. Pour over the Margarita and stir. Repeat with the remaining ingredients.

tapas and sherry

menu for 6

Although this is essentially a drinks party with snacks, you can actually offer some quite substantial food—what the Spanish would refer to as "raciones." As with other menus, you can buy many of the dishes—see page 71 for my store-bought suggestions—but there are some great recipes here that I use regularly, to add to your repertoire. As I love sherry, this is one of my favorite ways of entertaining.

albondigas

zucchini, potato, and onion tortilla

braised fava beans with pancetta and mint

mixed seafood salad with lemon, caper,
and parsley dressing

TO DRINK A chilled fino manzanilla sherry would go well with all these savory tapas. Alternatively, you could offer Spain's famous sparkling wine, Cava, a dry Spanish 'rosado', unoaked white Rioja or Rueda, or even a Spanish beer.

Spanish-style orange and almond cake

TO DRINK Serve a sweet oloroso sherry or a sherry-based orange liqueur.

albondigas (meatballs)

I adore meatballs of any description, so this is one of my favorite tapas. They are time-consuming, but children will love helping you make them—and can eat any leftovers!

3 tablespoons Spanish extra virgin olive oil

½ bunch of scallions, trimmed and very thinly sliced or 1 small onion, very finely chopped

3 garlic cloves, crushed

14 oz. spicy pork sausages

16 oz. lean ground beef

½ cup pimento-stuffed green olives, very finely chopped

2 tablespoons very finely chopped flatleaf parsley

2–3 tablespoons all-purpose flour

4–5 tablespoons sunflower or light olive oil

½ teaspoon sweet (dulce) Spanish pimentón or paprika

2 cups tomato purée or passata

sea salt and freshly ground black pepper

a roasting pan or ovenproof dish
toothpicks

Serves 8

Preheat the oven to 375°F. Heat a large skillet over medium heat and add 2 tablespoons of the olive oil. Fry the scallions and 2 garlic cloves for a couple of minutes without coloring until soft and set aside. Slit and pull away the skins of the sausages, put the sausagemeat in a large bowl with the ground beef and mix together thoroughly (hands are easiest, but you can use a fork and/or a wooden spoon.) Add the softened scallions and garlic, olives, and parsley, season with salt and pepper and mix again until all the ingredients are thoroughly amalgamated.

Sprinkle some of the flour over a cutting board. Lightly flour your hands before taking heaping teaspoonfuls of the meat mixture and rolling them between your palms into small meatballs. Flour your board and hands again as necessary. Wipe the skillet with paper towels and put back on the heat. Add 3 tablespoons of the oil and fry the meatballs in batches, browning them on all sides, adding extra oil if needed. Put the meatballs in the roasting pan or ovenproof dish as you finish them.

Discard any remaining oil in the pan, rinse clean and wipe with paper towels. Replace over the heat. Add the remaining oil, garlic, and the pimentón, stir for a few seconds and tip in the tomato purée. Cook for 2–3 minutes, then check the seasoning, adding salt and pepper to taste. Pour the sauce over the meatballs and bake in the preheated oven for 35–40 minutes until they are nicely browned, turning them in the sauce halfway through the cooking time. Serve warm on toothpicks.

zucchini, potato, and onion tortilla

Tortilla is one of those dishes that is really straightforward, but hard to make it taste as it did on vacation in Spain. The secret is patience, as it needs a good deal more time than a conventional omelet.

7 tablespoons Spanish extra virgin olive oil

3 medium or 2 large zucchini, cut into slices about ½ inch thick

12 oz. waxy potatoes, very thinly sliced*

1 large Spanish onion, very thinly sliced

1 heaping teaspoon finely chopped thyme (optional)

8 eggs, lightly beaten

sea salt and freshly ground black pepper

a wok
a deep-sided, non-stick skillet, about 9–10 inches wide

Serves 6–8

Heat a wok over medium heat, add 3 tablespoons of the olive oil and stir-fry the zucchini slices until lightly browned (about 5 minutes.) Remove them from the pan with a slotted spoon, leaving behind as much of the oil as possible, and set aside. Add another 3 tablespoons of oil to the pan, heat for a minute, then tip in the potato slices and stir with a spatula to ensure they are separate and well coated with oil. Fry, stirring, for about 5–6 minutes until they start to brown, then turn the heat down, cover the pan and cook for another 10–15 minutes until the potatoes are tender, turning them every so often to ensure they don't catch. Remove them from the pan, again leaving behind as much oil as possible. Add a little more oil if necessary, then add the onion and stir-fry for about 6–7 minutes until soft and beginning to brown. Add the thyme, then tip the other ingredients back into the pan, mix together lightly and season well with salt and pepper. Tip the vegetables into the beaten eggs and mix well.

Heat the deep-sided skillet until moderately hot, add a little oil, wipe off the excess with paper towels, then pour in the egg mixture. Lift the vegetables up around the edge of the pan to allow the liquid egg to trickle down to the base until most of the egg is set, then turn the heat down a little and leave the tortilla to cook for about 5 minutes while you preheat the broiler to moderate. Slip the skillet under the broiler about 5 inches from the heat until the egg on top of the tortilla is puffed up and lightly browned and the egg in the middle of the tortilla has set (about another 5–6 minutes.) Leave the tortilla to cool in the skillet, then loosen it around the edges. Put a plate over the skillet and flip the tortilla over so that it lands bottom-side upwards. Cut into slices or wedges and serve at room temperature.

* As you slice the potatoes, put them in a bowl of ice water to get rid of the excess starch, then give them a good swirl, drain off the water and dry them with paper towels.

braised fava beans with pancetta and mint

A delicious and easy tapas that goes particularly well with the meatballs or the Spanish air-dried ham Serrano. You can obviously make this with fresh fava beans in season, but the frozen ones are excellent and cut down cooking time.

3 tablespoons extra virgin olive oil

1 onion, finely chopped

3 oz. cubed pancetta

1–2 large garlic cloves, crushed

½ teaspoon sweet (dulce) Spanish pimentón or ¼ teaspoon paprika

16 oz. frozen baby fava beans

½ pint hot vegetable stock

1 heaping tablespoon chopped flatleaf parsley

1 heaping tablespoon chopped mint leaves

sea salt and freshly ground black pepper

Serves 6–8

Heat a skillet or flameproof casserole over medium heat, add 2 tablespoons of the olive oil and the onion and pancetta and fry gently for about 4–5 minutes until the onion is soft. Add the crushed garlic and pimentón, stir, then tip in the fava beans. Pour in the hot stock and bring to a boil, then cook for about 10 minutes until the beans are tender.

Take off the heat, cool for about 8–10 minutes, then add the herbs and remaining olive oil. Check the seasoning, adding salt and pepper to taste. Serve at room temperature.

mixed seafood salad with lemon, caper, and parsley dressing

A mixed pack of seafood makes the basis for this easy seafood salad, which goes fabulously well with chilled manzanilla sherry.

4 tablespoons Spanish extra virgin olive oil

1 large garlic clove, crushed

8 oz. mixed seafood cocktail, thawed if frozen

8 oz. small shelled shrimp, thawed if frozen

2 teaspoons finely grated lemon zest

1½–2 tablespoons freshly squeezed lemon juice

2 tablespoons capers, rinsed and finely chopped

3 tablespoons finely chopped flatleaf parsley

sea salt and freshly ground black pepper

Serves 6

Heat a large skillet over medium heat, add the olive oil and garlic and fry for a few seconds, then tip in the seafood cocktail and shrimp. Turn the heat up and stir-fry for a couple of minutes so that the seafood heats right through.

Remove from the heat and add the grated lemon zest, lemon juice, and capers and most of the parsley, saving a few leaves for garnishing. Mix together lightly and thoroughly. Check the seasoning adding salt and pepper to taste and extra lemon juice or olive oil if you think it needs it. Let cool, then cover and refrigerate for a few hours to allow the flavors to amalgamate.

Spanish-style orange and almond cake

This featherlight, syrup-drenched orange and almond cake, makes an impressive finale to a tapas meal.

4 large eggs, separated

1 heaping tablespoon finely grated orange zest

½ cup superfine

¾ cup ground almonds, sifted

1 teaspoon orange-flower water

For the syrup:

freshly squeezed juice of 1½ oranges and 1 lemon (about ½ cup juice in total)

6 tablespoons superfine or granulated sugar

1 cinnamon stick

½ teaspoon orange-flower water

an 8-inch cake pan, lined with a round of baking parchment

Serves 8–10

Preheat the oven to 350°F. Put the egg yolks in a large bowl with the orange zest and all except 1 tablespoon of the sugar and beat well, until light and moussey (about 2–3 minutes.) Fold in a third of the almonds, then the next third and finally the remaining third. (The mixture will be quite thick, but don't worry!) Wash and dry the beaters thoroughly. Whisk the egg whites in a separate bowl until just stiff, then add the remaining sugar and briefly whisk again. Take a couple of spoonfuls of the meringue and fold it into the cake mixture to loosen it. Fold in half the remaining meringue then, when the mixture is quite loose, carefully fold in the final portion, taking care not to overmix. Spoon the cake mixture into the prepared pan and bake for about 40–45 minutes until the surface of the cake is well browned and firm and the cake has shrunk away from the side of the pan. Remove from the oven and let cool for 5 minutes, then turn out on a wire rack.

While the cake is cooking, make the syrup. Put the orange and lemon juices in a small saucepan, add the sugar, cinnamon stick, and orange flower water and heat gently, stirring occasionally, until all the grains of sugar have dissolved. Bring to a boil and boil without stirring for about 4–5 minutes. Strain and cool. After the cake has cooled for about 15 minutes, put it upside-down on a plate, pierce it in several places with a skewer and spoon over some of the syrup a tablespoonful at a time. Carefully turn the cake over, pierce the top of the cake and spoon over as much of the remaining syrup as the cake will absorb. Let finish cooling before serving.

* You can dress this up into a dessert by serving the cake with some sliced caramelized oranges and a spoonful of whipped, sweetened cream flavored with a few drops of orange-flower water.

deli-bought tapas

You can buy everything you need to put together a selection of Spanish-style tapas in a gourmet store or deli these days: fine slices of serrano or (even better) Pata Negra (acorn-fed ham), chorizo, thin slices of Manchego cheese, toasted and salted Marcona almonds, large caper berries, marinated olives, and piquillo peppers, which taste good warmed through with a little olive oil and garlic, prepared as follows:-

Warm a couple of large spoonfuls of good olive oil over low heat. Add a few very finely sliced garlic cloves and keep over low heat for about 10 minutes without allowing them to color. Drain a jar or can of red piquillo peppers, quarter the peppers and warm them through in the garlic-infused oil. Serve with crusty bread on the side to mop up the juices.

deli-bought dessert tapas

It is equally easy to put together a Spanish-inspired "dessert tapas" selection including turrón (Spanish nougat, which comes in a variety of versions, including hard and soft), Spanish cookies, such as hazelnut Polvorónes, or Ines Rosáles tortas de aceite and anis (deliciously crispy aniseed and olive oil biscuits), dried fruits such as figs, and large moscatel raisins, an almond cake (or make the one opposite), and maybe some Spanish chocolates. You could partner them with a sweet oloroso sherry, good coffee, and Spanish brandy.

Another easy, delicious idea is to serve scoops of store-bought vanilla ice cream with ultra-rich, syrupy PX (Pedro Ximenez) sherry trickled over the top.

cooling food for a hot evening

menu for 6

It might seem a contradiction to suggest that the ideal food to serve on a sultry evening is spicy food, but if you think about those countries that habitually have hot weather like India or Thailand, you realize that that is exactly what you need. What you will also notice is that they serve it lukewarm or cold so that the heat doesn't become overwhelming. This is an eclectic modern menu to serve to adventurous friends who love new tastes and flavors.

ginger and lemongrass Martinis

TO DRINK Kick the evening off with a fragrant Martini; cocktails are always good on a hot evening. You can make a non-alcoholic version for those who don't drink or serve one of the refreshing new green tea-based drinks.

spiced mango, carrot, and chile soup

Thai-style beef with tomato and herb salad
shrimp and cucumber sesame noodles

TO DRINK With the soup and salads I suggest a dry aromatic white like an Alsace Riesling, an Austrian Grüner Veltliner or a limey Australian Verdelho. A Belgian witbier (cloudy wheat beer) would also work well.

exotic fruits with Piña Colada sherbet

spiced mango, carrot, and chile soup

An unusual and stunning-looking chilled soup that is wonderfully refreshing on a warm evening. Make sure your mango is ripe or you won't get the depth of flavor you need. You might want a slightly less ripe one for the garnish.

3 tablespoons grapeseed or vegetable oil

1 onion, roughly chopped

4 carrots, thinly sliced

½ teaspoon ground turmeric

1 teaspoon grated fresh ginger or ginger paste

1 pint vegetable stock

2 large, ripe mangoes, peeled and diced

freshly squeezed juice of 1–1½ limes (3–4 tablespoons)

sea salt and cayenne pepper

To serve:

low-fat plain yogurt

1 small mango, peeled and cut into small dice, to serve

Thai sweet chile sauce

a small bunch of cilantro

Japanese rice crackers, to serve (optional)

Serves 4–6

Heat the oil over low heat in a large, lidded skillet or flameproof casserole. Add the onion, stir, cover and cook gently for 5 minutes. Add the carrots, stir, replace the lid and continue to cook for another 10 minutes. Stir in the turmeric and ginger, cook for a minute then pour in the vegetable stock. Bring to a boil and simmer until the carrot is cooked—about 20 minutes. Set aside until cool (about an hour.)

Strain off the liquid into a bowl and tip the vegetables into a food processor along with the mango pieces. Add 2–3 tablespoons of the liquid and whizz until smooth. Add half the remaining liquid and whizz again. Tip the purée into the bowl with the rest of the liquid and mix well. Add 3 tablespoons of the lime juice and season with salt and cayenne pepper. Cover and refrigerate for at least 2 hours.

To serve, pour in enough ice water to create a thin, spoonable consistency. Check the seasoning, adding extra lime juice to taste if needed. Ladle the soup into bowls and spoon over a swirl of yogurt. Scatter with a few cubes of mango, drizzle over a little sweet chile sauce, and scatter with cilantro leaves. Serve with Japanese rice crackers on the side.

Thai-style beef with tomato and herb salad

Thai cuisine features some great meat-based salads that are wonderfully zingy and refreshing. The amount of chile you use is up to you. You can leave out the roasted chiles and only use fresh ones if you like, but I like the smoky flavor they give.

2 tablespoons Thai fragrant rice

1 teaspoon crushed chiles

1–2 thick slices of rump steak (about 2 lbs. in total and about 1-inch thick), trimmed of fat

1½ tablespoons sunflower or light olive oil

3–4 teaspoons superfine sugar

freshly squeezed juice of 3 limes, about 7–9 tablespoons

4 tablespoons Thai fish sauce

2 large garlic cloves, grated

2–3 medium-hot fresh red chiles, seeded and very finely chopped

8 small shallots, very thinly sliced
or a bunch of scallions, trimmed and thinly sliced

5 heaping tablespoons cilantro leaves, chopped

3 heaping tablespoons mint leaves, chopped

8 oz. cherry tomatoes, quartered

1 romaine lettuce heart, washed and crisped in the fridge

a ridged, stovetop grill pan

Serves 6–8

Heat a small skillet over medium heat, add the rice and cook, stirring occasionally until golden and fragrant (about 5 minutes). Take off the heat, allow to cool for a couple of minutes, then grind in a mortar with a pestle or the end of a rolling pin. Toast the crushed chiles in the same way for a few seconds, add to the rice and grind again. Heat a ridged, stovetop grill pan for about 3 minutes until smoking hot, rub the steak the oil and cook for about 1½ minutes each side until charred but still rare (or longer if you prefer.) Set aside to cool while you make the dressing.

Dissolve the sugar in the lime juice, add the fish sauce, the garlic, and half the chopped chiles and taste. Add more fish sauce and chiles if you think the dressing needs it and a little water if the dressing is too strong. Slice the steak thinly, then tip the slices together with any juices into a bowl with the dressing and add the shallots, cilantro, mint, and tomatoes. Toss, then sprinkle with the toasted rice. Finely shred the lettuce and arrange the shredded leaves on a large platter. Top with the dressed beef to serve.

shrimp and cucumber sesame noodles

A clean, refreshing noodle salad that goes particularly well with the beef.

8 oz. fine rice or dried soba noodles

14 oz. cooked shelled shrimp, thawed if frozen

⅔ cucumber, peeled, quartered, seeded and cut into diagonal slices

½ bunch of scallions, trimmed and thinly sliced

For the dressing:

6 tablespoons Japanese seasoned rice vinegar

2 tablespoons light soy sauce

4 tablespoons sunflower or rapeseed oil

2 tablespoons sesame oil

1½ teaspoons finely grated fresh ginger

1½ teaspoons finely grated garlic

4 tablespoons toasted sesame seeds*

5 tablespoons finely chopped cilantro leaves

sea salt (optional)

Serves 6–8

Break the dried noodles into thirds and put them in a heatproof bowl. Pour over boiling water, leave for 3 minutes, then drain and rinse under cold water. Put them in a large serving bowl and add the shrimp, cucumber, and scallions.

Pour the rice vinegar and soy sauce into a separate bowl, then whisk in the sunflower oil and sesame oil. Whisk in the ginger and garlic, add the dressing to the noodles and toss together. Check the seasoning, adding a little salt if necessary. Just before serving, sprinkle over the sesame seeds and cilantro and toss again.

*To toast the sesame seeds, warm them in a dry skillet over low heat until they begin to change color.

exotic fruits

Make up a large, attractive platter of exotic fruits such as pineapple, mango, papaya, passion fruit, star fruit, kiwis, and lychees so that your guests can help themselves.

Piña Colada sherbet

This is a cross between an ice cream and a sorbet. It makes a fantastically refreshing end to the meal. Don't make it more than a few days in advance, as it won't keep like a commercial ice cream.

¾ cup superfine or granulated sugar

1 ripe pineapple

¾ cup coconut cream

6 tablespoons freshly squeezed lime juice (2–3 limes)

4 tablespoons white rum

2 large egg whites, beaten

Serves 6–8

Put the sugar in a pan with ¾ cup water over very low heat, stirring occasionally, until the sugar has dissolved. Bring to a boil without stirring and boil for about 4 minutes. Set aside to cool. Quarter the pineapple, cut away the tough central core and cut off the skin. Cut into cubes and pass through a juicer.* This should give you about 2½ cups juice. Mix in the coconut cream, cooled sugar syrup, lime juice, and rum, which should give you just over 1 quart liquid.

Cover, transfer the sherbet mixture to the fridge and chill for a couple of hours. Pour into an ice cream machine and churn, adding the egg whites halfway through. (You may need to do this in 2 batches.) If you haven't got an ice cream machine, pour the sherbet mix into a lidded freezerproof container and freeze for about 1½ hours or until beginning to harden at the edges. Put the egg whites in a food processor, process briefly until frothy, then tip in the half-frozen sherbet mixture and whizz until smooth. Return the sherbet mix to the freezer, freeze for another hour, then whizz again. Freeze and whizz a third time for extra smoothness. Leave to harden. Before serving, remove the sherbet from the freezer and leave to mellow in the fridge for about 20 minutes. Serve with a selection of tropical fruits.

* If you haven't got a juicer, remove all the little brown "eyes" from the pineapple, cut into cubes, purée in a food processor and strain the juice.

ginger and lemongrass Martinis

Bottled cordials make rustling up a cocktail incredibly easy. You can vary the quantities depending how gingery or how sweet you like your drinks, but this works for me.

crushed ice

1 shot ginger and lemongrass cordial

2 shots vodka

a thinly pared slice of lemon zest

a short length of lemongrass stalk, outer layer removed, to garnish

a Martini glass

Serves 1

Fill a cocktail shaker with ice. Add the cordial and vodka and shake well. Strain into a Martini glass. Holding the piece of lemon zest, twist it over the drink so the lemon oil in the zest drops on the surface then drop it into the drink. Garnish with the lemongrass.

a farmers' market dinner

menu for 6

There's nothing more inspirational than a visit to the local farmers' market, especially in spring when the new season's vegetables finally arrive after the bleak stretch of winter. Invite friends over to share the bounty the same evening and enjoy the produce at its freshest and best.

pea and Parma ham crostini

farmers' market salad with goat cheese,
asparagus and roast beets

spring vegetable pasta with lemon

strawberry, rose, and rhubarb fool

TO DRINK At this time of year I like to keep the drink light and white. The green sappy, citrussy flavours of Sauvignon Blanc are a perfect choice with the first two courses of this menu. I'd choose one from the Loire like a Sancerre or Pouilly Fumé. With the pasta, I'd serve a good Italian Pinot Grigio or a Chablis. You could offer non-drinkers an elderflower spritzer.

farmers' market salad with goat cheese, asparagus, and roast beets

This salad came about a couple of years ago as a result of a visit to my local farmers' market and has remained a firm favorite ever since. Don't let memories of vinegar-soused beets put you off—roast beets have a fabulously sweet, earthy flavor that just needs a few salad greens and some fresh tangy goat cheese to set it off.

a bunch of fresh beets

4 tablespoons sunflower oil

2 lbs. fava bean pods

a bunch of fresh asparagus

3 tablespoons rice vinegar

2 tablespoons walnut oil

2 generous handfuls mixed salad greens, such as arugula, watercress, baby spinach, or mustard leaves

7 oz. goat cheese

a small handful of chopped green herbs, such as parsley or dill

a few chives, snipped

sea salt and freshly ground black pepper

Serves 4–6

Preheat the oven to 400°F. Cut off the beet tops and trim off the roots. Wash the beet under running water to remove any dirt and dry with paper towels. Take a large piece of foil and place it on a baking sheet. Oil it lightly, place the beet in the centre and scrunch the edges of the foil together to make a loose tent. Cook in the preheated oven for 50 minutes–1 hour or until tender. When cool enough to handle, peel off the skins and cut into wedges.

Meanwhile, shell the fava and cook them in boiling water for about 8–10 minutes or until just cooked. When cool enough to handle, pop the beans out of their skins. Cut the tips of the asparagus off about a third of the way down the stalk and steam or microwave for about 3–4 minutes until just tender. Set aside and let cool.

Shake the vinegar, oils, salt, and pepper together in a screw-top glass jar. Use half to lightly dress the wedges of beet. Divide the leaves between 4 plates and drizzle with a little of the remaining dressing. Arrange the beet over the leaves and top with roughly torn chunks of goat cheese and the fava beans. Scatter over the herbs, trickle over the remaining dressing and grind a little black pepper over the top. Serve with some crusty bread.

pea and Parma ham crostini

The new season's peas are so deliciously sweet that you want to enjoy them every which way you can.

2 cups shelled fresh or frozen peas

2 scallions

1/3 cup finely grated aged pecorino or Parmesan cheese

1 tablespoon finely chopped mint or dill

2 tablespoons fruity olive oil

18 ciabatta toasts (see page 28)

4 oz. thinly sliced Parma ham or other air-dried ham, torn or cut in half

salt and freshly ground black pepper

freshly squeezed lemon juice, to taste

Makes 18 crostini

Cook the peas in boiling water for 2–3 minutes or until just tender. Drain under cold running water. Trim and cut the scallions in half lengthways, then slice very thinly.

Put the peas and onions in a food processor and pulse until you get a chunky spread. Add the pecorino and mint and pulse again, then stir in the olive oil. Season to taste with salt, pepper, and lemon juice. Spread the mixture thickly on ciabatta toasts and drape with a piece of ham. Serve immediately.

spring vegetable pasta with lemon

This dish is admittedly more vegetable than pasta, but it's one of the most delicious ways to enjoy the new season's produce. You can vary the vegetables depending on what's available. Baby zucchini also work well, as does fennel. The key thing is to cook them until they're only just done to preserve their delicate flavor and bright green color.

a small bunch of asparagus
1 cup shelled fresh peas
a few stalks of sprouting broccoli
5 oz. fava beans
7 tablespoons butter
1 leek or ½ bunch of scallions, thinly sliced
1¼ cups heavy cream
10 oz. dried egg pasta shapes, such as Campanelle
freshly squeezed juice of 2–3 lemons (about ½ cup)
3 heaping tablespoons finely chopped parsley
2 heaping tablespoons each finely chopped dill and snipped chives
sea salt and freshly ground black pepper
freshly shaved Parmesan cheese or grana padano, to serve

Serves 6

Snap the asparagus spears two-thirds down the stalks and discard the woody ends. Cut the remaining stem into short lengths. Steam or microwave them for about 2–3 minutes until just cooked and refresh with ice water. Repeat with the other vegetables—steaming them individually until just cooked. (Pop the fava beans out of their skins for an even sweeter taste.)

Gently melt the butter in a large saucepan or flameproof casserole and cook the leek for a couple of minutes until starting to soften. Tip in the other vegetables, lightly toss with the butter, cover the pan and leave over very low heat, adding the cream once the vegetables have heated through.

Cook the pasta following the instructions on the packet. Reserve a little of the cooking water and drain well. Tip the drained pasta into the vegetables and toss together. Add the lemon juice and herbs, season with salt and pepper and toss together lightly. Check the seasoning, adding extra salt, pepper, lemon juice, or a little of the reserved pasta cooking water to lighten the sauce if you think it needs it. Serve in warm bowls with shavings of Parmesan.

strawberry, rose, and rhubarb fool

Rhubarb and strawberries have an extraordinary affinity and fortunately come into season at the same time of year.

14 oz. fresh rhubarb
3 tablespoons superfine or granulated sugar
1½ cups fresh, ripe strawberries, plus a few extra to garnish
2–3 tablespoons rose syrup or rosewater and extra caster sugar
1¼ cups Greek yogurt
1¼ cups whipping cream

6 glasses or glass serving dishes

Serves 6

Slice the rhubarb and put it in a saucepan with the sugar and 2 tablespoons water. Put a lid on the pan and heat over low heat until the fruit comes to a boil, then turn the heat down and simmer for 7–10 minutes until the fruit is soft. Tip the fruit into a sieve over a bowl and drain off the juice.

Hull the strawberries, put them in a food processor and whizz until smooth. Add the drained rhubarb and 1 tablespoon rose syrup or 2 teaspoons rosewater with 1 tablespoon sugar and whizz again. Tip the purée into a bowl and leave to cool. Tip the yogurt into a large bowl. In a separate bowl, whip the cream until just holding its shape and sweeten to taste with rose syrup or rosewater and sugar. Fold half the cream into the yogurt. Fold half the puréed strawberry and rhubarb into the yogurt and cream mixture then lightly mix the remaining cream and the rest of the rhubarb and strawberry purée to create a marbled effect.

Spoon the fool into individual glasses and chill until ready to serve. Slice the remaining strawberries and sprinkle with a few drops of rose syrup or a little sugar. Use the strawberry slices to decorate the top of each glass.

Time-saving tip: If you don't have time to make a dessert, simply serve some early-season strawberries with pouring cream. You'll probably need to sweeten them a touch at this time of year: slice and sprinkle them with caster sugar then leave them to macerate for 15–20 minutes before serving them.

Moroccan-inspired summer feast

menu for 6

I love the gentle, subtle spicy flavors of Moroccan food, the exquisite balance between vegetables, meat, fruit, and grain. The recipes are more time consuming to prepare than many in this book, admittedly, but this is a pleasurable meal to make with family or friends who share your passion for cooking.

spiced carrot and black olive salad
eggplant and tomato salad
grilled bell pepper, tomato, and chile salad

chicken, lemon, and green olive tagine

zucchini and mint couscous

orange-flower water salad

Moroccan mint tea and pastries

TO DRINK Most Moroccans do not drink alcohol, so a fruit juice like pomegranate juice would be an appropriate accompaniment to this meal, served in a large pitcher with ice and slices of lime. Wine-wise I'd go for a light, dry rosé such as a southern French Syrah rosé, a Spanish rosado, or a mature oak-aged Spanish red like a Rioja Reserva.

The gentle aromatic spicing of these three Moroccan cooked salads is just perfect for a warm evening. You can prepare them well ahead. Serve with warmed flatbreads or pita bread.

spiced carrot and black olive salad

12 oz. baby carrots

2 tablespoons olive oil

$\frac{1}{2}$ teaspoon Moroccan spice mix*

a pinch each of sea salt and sugar

$2\frac{1}{2}$ oz. pitted black olives marinated with herbs

freshly squeezed juice of $\frac{1}{2}$ orange (about 2 tablespoons)

a good squeeze of lemon juice

$\frac{1}{2}$ teaspoon lightly crushed roasted cumin seeds** (optional)

2 tablespoons chopped cilantro

Serves 6

Cut the carrots into thin diagonal slices. Heat the oil in a saucepan over low heat, add the spice mix, and cook for a few seconds. Tip in the carrots, turn them in the spiced oil and cook gently for 3–4 minutes. Stir in the salt and sugar, add 2 tablespoons water and put a lid on the pan. Cook the carrots over low heat until they are soft (about 20 minutes), stirring occasionally and adding a little more water if the carrots start to burn.

Tip the carrots into a dish, cool, then mix in the olives and orange juice. Season to taste with salt and lemon juice. Just before serving, sprinkle over the cumin seeds, if using, and chopped cilantro.

* I make my own Moroccan-style spice mix in small batches: 2 tablespoons each of ground cumin and ground coriander, 2 teaspoons turmeric and 1–1$\frac{1}{2}$ teaspoons chile powder or hot (piquante) pimentón.

** To roast cumin seeds, put them in a small skillet over a gentle heat and warm them through until they begin to change color and smell fragrant.

eggplant and tomato salad

2 medium or 1 large eggplant

4 tablespoons olive oil

1 onion, roughly chopped

1 garlic clove, crushed

2 tomatoes, peeled*, seeded and diced

2 tablespoons chopped parsley

1 tablespoon chopped mint leaves

1–1$\frac{1}{2}$ tablespoons freshly squeezed lemon juice

1 teaspoon ground cumin

sea salt and freshly ground black pepper

a lidded wok

Serves 6

Slice off the eggplant stalks and cut each eggplant in half lengthways and then into cubes. Heat a wok for about 2 minutes over high heat, add the oil and heat for a few seconds, then tip in the eggplant.

Stir-fry over medium heat for about 5 minutes until lightly browned, then turn the heat down slightly, add the onion and cook for another few minutes. Turn the heat down very low, stir in the garlic, cover the wok and cook gently for a further 10–12 minutes, stirring occasionally.

Tip the eggplant into a shallow dish and leave to cool for about 20 minutes. Mix in the tomato, parsley, and mint. Season with the lemon juice and cumin and salt and pepper to taste.

pepper, tomato, and chile salad

2 green bell peppers

3–4 long sweet red bell peppers

14 oz. ripe tomatoes, peeled*

$\frac{1}{4}$ teaspoon smoked sweet (dulce) pimentón or paprika

$\frac{1}{4}$ teaspoon ground cumin

1 tablespoon freshly squeezed lemon juice

2 tablespoons olive oil

2 tablespoons pickled sliced Jalapeño chiles, rinsed and finely chopped

1 heaping tablespoon finely chopped parsley

sea salt and freshly ground black pepper

Serves 6

To peel the bell peppers, either lay them over a low gas flame, turning frequently until the skins char, or halve them, lay them skin-side upwards on a broiler pan and broil under high heat until the skins are blackened. Put the charred peppers in a bowl and cover with plastic wrap. (This helps to loosen the skins.) Once the peppers are cool, rinse and rub them under cold running water, and the skins should slip off.

Seed the peppers, slice them thickly and put in a serving bowl with the tomatoes. Measure the pimentón and cumin into another small bowl and whisk in the lemon juice and oil. Season to taste with salt and pepper. Pour the dressing over the peppers, add the Jalapeños and parsley and toss together.

*To peel the tomatoes, make a small cut near the stalk of each one with a sharp knife, put them in a heatproof bowl and pour over boiling water. Leave for a minute, then pour the water away and cover the tomatoes with cold water. The skins should peel off easily.

wine and chocolate

Chocolate isn't the easiest ingredient to match with wine, but a sweet red like Maury is generally much more successful than a sweet white. Other reds you could consider include Mavrodaphne of Patras from Greece, Banyuls, which like Maury is from the South of France, Recioto from Italy or late-bottled vintage port, especially if there are some dark berry fruits like cherries in the dessert. See also page 140.

chocolate pots with Maury

It's so easy to buy great chocolate desserts these days that if you're going to make them yourself you need to give them a bit of a twist. Here I've added the French red dessert wine Maury, a wonderful accompaniment for chocolate. It's very rich but chocoholics will probably want two!

7 oz. premium bittersweet chocolate (minimum 70% cocoa solids)

1 cup Maury or ¾ cup late-bottled vintage port

1¼ cups whipping cream

2 very fresh large organic egg yolks* (optional)

1–2 tablespoons superfine sugar

cocoa powder and confectioners' sugar, to decorate

8–10 small ramekins or espresso cups

Serves 8–10

Break the chocolate into squares, put them in a food processor and briefly blitz them to break them into small pieces. Leave them in the processor.

Heat the Maury until almost at a boil and pour it over the chocolate. Heat the cream, until almost at a boil, and pour that over too. Leave for a few seconds to melt the chocolate, then whizz until the chocolate is smooth. Add the egg yolks and whizz again. Check for sweetness, adding sugar to taste. Pour the mixture into the serving dishes and chill in the fridge for a couple of hours, removing the desserts 20 minutes before serving. Using a small tea strainer, sift a thin layer of cocoa powder over the top of each pot, then follow with a sprinkling of confectioners' sugar.

* This dessert contains raw egg. It improves the texture, but you could leave it out if you prefer.

sheep cheese with cherry compôte

Rather than a full cheeseboard, you could serve slices of sheeps' milk cheese as they do in the south-west of France with a store-bought cherry compôte, a combination that works much better with red wine than cheese alone. Serve with thin slices of sourdough or whole-wheat bread.

a vegetarian harvest dinner

menu for 6

This is a simple dinner combining the best of fall's produce with a couple of
convenience products. Ready-made puff pastry has made it wonderfully easy to knock
up a quick, impressive tart, while a simple dessert of baked or broiled fruit dresses up a
store-bought tub of ice cream. The soup can be made ahead and frozen if you like.

pumpkin soup with honey and sage

TO DRINK Maybe I make a case for artisanal cider here? It is undergoing something of a
renaissance at the moment. Or perry, which is cider made with pears. I'd pick a medium dry
rather than a very dry one, which should take you right through the first two courses of this menu.
Alternatively, choose a lightly oaked Chardonnay.

heirloom tomato, bell pepper, and mozzarella tart

steamed new potatoes with butter, parsley, and chives

garden salad

TO DRINK A cider or perry (see above), or a soft, fruity red like Merlot would work here.

broiled figs with cinnamon and sweet sherry
brandy snaps

TO DRINK As these desserts already include a full-bodied sweet sherry and are served with ice
cream (which isn't the easiest ingredient to match with wine), I wouldn't suggest serving a
dessert wine with either.

pumpkin soup with honey and sage

This is based on a delicious soup I had at a restaurant called Tom's Kitchen, run by top London chef Tom Aikens. His version, I discovered, contained chicken stock. Mine is vegetarian, but you could base it on chicken stock too.

5 tablespoons unsalted butter
1 small–medium onion, roughly chopped
1 carrot, finely chopped
1 garlic clove, crushed
2¼ lbs. pumpkin or butternut squash, seeded, peeled and cut into cubes
2 heaping tablespoons clear honey
3 sprigs of sage, plus extra crisp-fried leaves (optional), to serve
3 cups vegetable stock
⅓ cup heavy cream
freshly squeezed lemon juice, to taste
sea salt and freshly ground black pepper

Serves 4–6

Gently melt the butter in a large lidded saucepan or flameproof casserole. Add the onion, carrot and garlic, stir, cover, and cook over low heat for about 4–5 minutes. Add the cubed pumpkin, honey and sage, stir, replace the lid and continue to cook very gently for about 10 minutes. Pour in the stock, bring to a boil and cook for a further 10 minutes until the vegetables are soft. Turn off the heat and allow the soup to cool slightly, then remove the sage and strain the soup, retaining the liquid. Put half the cooked vegetables in a food processor with just enough of the reserved cooking liquid to blend into a smooth purée.

Transfer to a clean saucepan and repeat with the remaining vegetables, adding the purée to the first batch. Whizz the remaining liquid in the food processor to pick up the last bits of purée and add that too. Bring the soup slowly to a boil, then stir in the cream without boiling further. Season to taste with lemon juice (about 1 tablespoon), salt (about a teaspoon) and pepper.

Serve with an extra swirl of cream or scatter some crisp-fried sage leaves on top and serve with whole-wheat or multigrain bread.

heirloom tomato, bell pepper, and mozzarella tart

There are so many beautifully colored tomatoes and peppers now, it's easy to make this spectacular-looking tart.

13 oz. ready-made puff pastry dough, thawed if frozen
1 large or 2 small red bell peppers
1 large or 2 small yellow bell peppers
3 tablespoons olive oil
2 garlic cloves, unpeeled and flattened
4 heaping tablespoons green or red pesto, homemade or from a jar
5½ oz. buffalo mozzarella, drained and thinly sliced
4 oz. red cherry tomatoes, destalked and halved
4 oz. yellow cherry tomatoes, destalked and halved
½ teaspoon dried oregano or marjoram
1 egg, lightly beaten
3 tablespoons grated or shaved Parmesan cheese
a few basil leaves, roughly torn
sea salt and freshly ground black pepper

a roasting pan
a rectangular baking sheet, lightly greased

Serves 4–6

Preheat the oven to 400°F. Take the pastry out of the fridge at least 20 minutes before you need to unroll it. Quarter the bell peppers, remove the pith and seeds and cut each quarter into half lengthways. Put them in a roasting pan with the garlic cloves, pour over 2 tablespoons of the oil and mix together well. Roast for about 20–25 minutes until the edges of the peppers are beginning to blacken. Remove and let cool for 10 minutes.

Roll out the pastry to a large rectangle and lay on the baking sheet. Using a sharp knife, score a line around the pastry about ½ inch from the edge. Spread the pesto evenly inside the rectangle you've marked. Lay the pepper strips across the base of the tart, alternating red and yellow sections. Distribute the mozzarella pieces over the peppers. Season with black pepper. Arrange the halved tomatoes over the peppers, red on yellow and yellow on red. Sprinkle the oregano over the tart, season with a little salt and a little more pepper and trickle over the remaining oil. Turn the oven up to 425°F. Brush the edges of the tart with the egg and bake for 12 minutes or until the edge of the tart is well puffed up and beginning to brown. Turn the heat back down again to 400°F and cook for another 12–15 minutes until the tops of the tomatoes are well browned. Sprinkle a little Parmesan over the tart, then let cool for 5 minutes. Scatter the basil over the tart to finish. Serve warm.

it's cold outside

(a midwinter dinner)

menu for 6

When it's cold outside, nothing is nicer than to sit around a candlelit table and enjoy
a nice meal. This menu is full of warm, comforting flavors—a smooth vegetable soup,
an old-fashioned pot roast served with gorgeous rich polenta, and an indulgent, creamy
dessert that's guaranteed to make you feel that the winter isn't so bad after all.

fennel, leek, and cauliflower soup

TO DRINK Soup isn't the easiest dish to pair with wine (two liquids together don't always work)
but the creamy texture of this soup goes well with a crisp, dry, fresh white such as a Chablis or
other unoaked white Burgundy.

pot roast brisket with Zinfandel
roast pumpkin and garlic polenta with cavolo nero

TO DRINK You want a robust, warming red—a good Zinfandel or a Cabernet Sauvignon would be
my top recommendations.

orange and Cointreau syllabub

TO DRINK I don't think this dessert needs an accompanying wine, but if you wanted to serve one,
a small glass of Australian botrytized Semillon would work well.

fennel, leek, and cauliflower soup

This deceptively creamy soup—which doesn't actually contain cream—is based on a delicious one made by Paul Hayes, the first chef at my son's London pub, The Marquess Tavern. Try if you can to use organic vegetables to make it: you really will be able to taste the difference.

2 tablespoons olive oil
2 tablespoons unsalted butter
2 leeks, trimmed and sliced
1 large or 2 small bulbs of fennel, trimmed and sliced
(reserve the feathery leaves if they're still on the bulb)
1 large garlic clove, crushed
1 small or ½ large cauliflower
1 quart fresh chicken or vegetable stock or made with
1 organic bouillon cube
1 bay leaf
2–3 sprigs tarragon or 1 teaspoon dried tarragon
2–3 tablespoons whole milk (optional)
a small pinch of mace
sea salt and freshly ground white or black pepper
a few fennel, dill or parsley leaves and some chives, to garnish

Serves 6

Heat the oil for a minute or two in a large saucepan, then add the butter. When the foaming dies down, add the leeks, fennel, and garlic, stir well, cover and cook over a low heat for about 8–10 minutes. Meanwhile, remove the florets from the cauliflower. Add them to the pan, stir and cook for another 3–4 minutes. Pour the stock over the vegetables, add the bay leaf and tarragon and bring to a boil. Partially cover the pan and simmer for about 15 minutes or until the cauliflower and fennel are soft. Remove from the heat and allow to cool slightly. Remove the bay leaf and tarragon. Strain the soup, reserving the liquid.

Put the vegetables in a food processor and whizz until smooth, adding as much of the reserved liquid as you need to make a smooth, creamy consistency. Whizz the remaining liquid in the blender or food processor to pick up the last scraps of vegetable purée and add to the soup in the pan. Reheat gently, diluting the soup with a little more stock or milk if it seems too thick. Season to taste with salt, pepper, and mace.

Chop the reserved fennel leaves or some dill or parsley and cut the chives into approximately 1-inch lengths. Serve the soup in individual bowls, scatter with the herbs and serve with some light rye or multigrain bread.

pot roast brisket with Zinfandel

Brisket is a much underrated cut with a rich flavor that lends itself well to braising. You can use any full-bodied red, but Zinfandel has just the right gutsy rustic character.

¾ cup Zinfandel or other full-bodied red wine
¾ cup fresh beef stock or stock made with ½ a bouillon cube, cooled
2 tablespoons red wine vinegar
1 large garlic clove, crushed
1 bay leaf
1 onion, chopped
a few of sprigs of thyme or ½ teaspoon dried thyme
3½ lbs. boned, rolled brisket of beef
2–3 tablespoons sunflower or light olive oil
2 tablespoons dry Marsala or Madeira
sea salt and freshly ground pepper

a flameproof casserole

Serves 6

Mix the wine and stock with the wine vinegar, garlic, bay leaf, onion, and thyme. Put the meat in a lock-tight plastic bag, pour over the marinade and close the bag tightly. The liquid should cover the meat. Leave the meat to marinate in the fridge for at least 4 hours or overnight.

Preheat the oven to 400°F. Remove the meat from the marinade and dry thoroughly with paper towels. Strain the marinade and reserve the liquid. Heat the oil in a flameproof casserole. Brown the meat all over in the hot oil then add 3–4 tablespoons of the strained marinade. Put a lid on the casserole and roast for 2 hours. Check from time to time that the pan juices are not burning. Add more marinade if necessary, but the flavor of this dish comes from the well-browned sticky juices, so do not add too much extra liquid. If on the other hand more liquid has formed, spoon some out. Simmer the remaining marinade over low heat until it loses its raw, winey taste.

Once the meat is cooked, set it aside in a warm place. Spoon any fat off the surface of the pan juices and add the Marsala and the cooked marinade. Bring to a boil, scraping off all the brown tasty bits from the side of the casserole and adding a little extra water if necessary. Season to taste with salt and pepper and serve spooned over slices of the meat or in a gravy boat for pouring.

a romantic Champagne dinner

menu for 2

The key to a romantic dinner is not to give yourself too much last-minute work or to eat or drink too much—unless you want to end up snoring on the sofa! Since you're probably going to open a bottle of Champagne at some point, you might as well drink it all the way through, which works well with this luxurious seafood-based menu.

~

warm scallop salad
with crispy pancetta and parsnip crisps
or
warm oysters with cucumber and Champagne

lobster and fries

Chaource with black truffles

passion fruit pavlovas

TO DRINK This menu is designed to be accompanied by Champagne and, if you can run to it, a vintage one. Choose a recent vintage rather than a very old one, as you may not like the complex yeasty flavors that mature Champagne acquires. An alternative would be to drink a glass of fizz with the oysters or scallops and move on to a top-quality Chardonnay with the lobster.

passion fruit pavlovas

A simple-to-assemble, fresh-tasting and impressive dessert.

2 ripe passion fruit

1 tablespoon freshly squeezed orange juice

1 teaspoon superfine or granulated sugar, plus extra to taste

a few drops of orange-flower water (optional)

2 store-bought meringue nests

2 heaping tablespoons lemon or orange curd (optional)

4 small scoops premium vanilla ice cream

Serves 2

Halve the passion fruit and scoop the pulp and seeds into a small bowl, taking care not to remove any of the bitter pith.

Add the orange juice and sugar and stir. Check for sweetness, adding the orange-flower water and/or extra sugar to taste.

Put a meringue nest on each plate and spoon the curd, if using, into the base. Top with the vanilla ice cream and spoon over the orange and passion fruit sauce.

Chaource with black truffle

This is a brilliant tip I got from American cookery writer Patricia Wells. Take a small, deep, round, soft white-rinded cow cheese, about 3 inches in diameter and about 1½–2 inches deep or half a slightly bigger one, such as Chaource (which comes from the Champagne region of France), and cut it horizontally into three slices (this is easier if it's chilled.) Thinly slice a black truffle, lay the slices between the layers, trickling over a few drops of black truffle-infused oil over the sliced truffles, and sandwich the layers together. Wrap tightly with plastic wrap and refrigerate for at least a day and preferably two days. Cut into wedges, bring to room temperature and serve with slices of sourdough or French baguette.

food and fizz

Sparkling wine is much more versatile with food than people think, its natural carbonation acting as a palate cleanser and appetite stimulant. Its lightness makes it a natural partner for raw or lightly cooked shellfish and other seafood, for light pastas and risottos, and with chicken.

Surprisingly, although it is regarded as a dry wine, you can also drink it with airy desserts such as cakes, soufflés, and meringues, and with red berry fruits such as strawberries and raspberries. You can also drink it with light creamy cheeses such as Chaource.

a festive winter dinner

menu for 6

Most of us have tried and trusted recipes for our Christmas or Thanksgiving dinner from which we wouldn't dare deviate, but there are many other meals to be catered for during the holiday season. They needn't be (thankfully) as time-consuming to prepare as The Big Meal itself, but they can be a lot more fun for the cook. You can mix and match the courses any way you like: follow the soup with the pumpkin pie or with cookies and mulled wine, or simply invite a few friends round for some egg nog and cookies.

chestnut and Puy lentil soup

with whipped celeriac cream

TO DRINK Choose a light unoaked Chardonnay such as Chablis or a neutral clean white such as Albariño. (If you don't make the celeriac topping, you could use a richer, oakier Chardonnay.)

winter cheeseboard (see page 138)

roast pumpkin and pecan pie

TO DRINK Muscats and Moscatels go particularly well with pumpkin pie—Australian liqueur Muscat if you have an exceptionally sweet tooth, a lighter Southern French or Spanish Muscat if you haven't. You could also try a sweet sherry or a young tawny port.

ginger and cinnamon thins
orange-mulled wine, mulled cider, or egg nog

chestnut and Puy lentil soup with whipped celeriac cream

This is a spectacularly rich, satisfying soup with a light-as-air, foamy topping. You can prepare the soup ahead and it's a particularly good way to use up a tasty turkey or ham stock. You don't have to peel your own chestnuts, but they do taste wonderful and it's a nice, cosy thing to do if you've got company in the kitchen. If you prefer to serve the soup on its own without the topping, save some of the chopped chestnut for garnishing, frying the pieces in a little butter before serving.

16 oz. whole chestnuts or 12 oz. ready-prepared chestnuts

4 tablespoons light olive oil

1 leek, trimmed and thinly sliced

1 large carrot, finely diced

1 celery rib, thinly sliced

1 garlic clove, crushed

1 teaspoon sweet (dulce) pimentón or paprika

1½–2 quarts fresh turkey, duck, ham, chicken or game stock or stock made with 2 organic bouillon cubes

1 cup French Puy lentils, rinsed

2 tablespoons dry Marsala, Madeira or amontillado sherry

½–1 teaspoon Worcestershire or dark soy sauce (optional)

sea salt and freshly ground black pepper

For the celeriac cream:

1 lb. celeriac

2⅓ cups low-fat milk (1%)

2 tablespoons butter

freshly grated nutmeg, to taste

a few snipped chives, to garnish

Serves 6–8

Wash the chestnuts and make a cut with a sharp knife in the curved side of each one. Put in a saucepan of boiling water, bring back to a boil and boil for 3 minutes. Turn the heat off and remove the chestnuts 2 at a time, letting them cool for a few seconds, then peeling off both the hard outer shell and inner brown papery skin. If they become harder to peel, bring the water back to a boil again. Chop them roughly.

Heat the oil in a large saucepan, add the leek, carrot, and celery, stir well and cook over medium heat until the vegetables start to soften (about 5–6 minutes.) Stir in the garlic and pimentón and cook for a minute, then add the chestnuts and 1 quart of the stock and bring to a boil. Add the lentils to the vegetables, then cook for about 35–40 minutes until the vegetables are soft. Cool for 10 minutes, then pass the soup in batches through a food processor. Return the soup and remaining stock to the pan, add the Marsala and reheat gently. Add more stock if necessary and season to taste with salt, pepper, and Worcestershire sauce.

Meanwhile, to make the celeriac cream, remove the tough outer skin from the celeriac and cut it into cubes. Put in a saucepan, add enough of the milk to cover and bring to a boil. Partially cover the pan and simmer for about 20–25 minutes, until the celeriac is soft. Remove the celeriac with a slotted spoon, leaving the liquid behind, and whizz it in a food processor. Season with salt, pepper, and a little freshly grated nutmeg. Remove half the purée and add half the remaining milk to the purée in the food processor. Whizz until smooth, light and foamy, adding a little extra milk if needed.

Serve the soup in bowls with a generous swirl of celeriac cream on the top and garnish with snipped chives. Serve with some crusty sourdough or multigrain bread.

roast pumpkin and pecan pie

This recipe may look slightly daunting, but I promise you it is worth the effort. Do roast the pumpkin if you're cooking it from scratch—it has a much better texture than when you boil it.

For the crust:
2 cups all-purpose flour
1 teaspoon ground ginger
2 tablespoons confectioners' sugar
1 stick butter, chilled and cut into cubes
2 tablespoons vegetable shortening
1 egg yolk (reserve the white)
a pinch of salt

For the pumpkin purée:
1 lb. roast pumpkin flesh (see method)
1 tablespoon bourbon or dark rum
1 tablespoon light brown sugar
1/4 teaspoon apple pie spice
1 tablespoon butter, chilled

For the pie filling:
1/2 cup light brown sugar
1 tablespoon maple syrup or clear honey
1 1/2 teaspoons apple pie spice
1/2 teaspoon ground cinnamon
a pinch of salt
1 tablespoon bourbon or dark rum
3 eggs

2 tablespoons all-purpose flour, sifted
2/3 cup heavy cream

For the topping:
1/3 cup pecan nuts
1 tablespoon light brown sugar

a 9-inch pie plate

Serves 6

First make the pie crust. Sift the flour, ginger, and confectioners' sugar into a large bowl. Cut the butter and shortening cubes into the flour, then rub with your fingertips until the mixture resembles coarse breadcrumbs. Mix the egg yolk with 2 tablespoons ice water, add to the bowl, mix lightly and pull together into a ball, adding extra water if needed. Shape into a flat disc, put in a plastic bag, and refrigerate for at least half an hour.

Preheat the oven to 400°F. To make the pumpkin purée, scrape away all the seeds and fibrous flesh surrounding them and cut into even-sized chunks. Put the chunks on a piece of lightly oiled foil. Sprinkle over the bourbon, sugar, and apple pie spice and dot with the chilled butter. Bring the foil up round the sides and fold over carefully to form a loose but airtight package. Place in a baking dish and cook in the preheated oven for 40 minutes until the pumpkin is soft. Carefully open up the foil, let cool for a few minutes, then tip the pumpkin and the juices into a food processor and whizz until smooth.

Roll out the pastry and line the pie plate. Trim the edges and press the base well into the pan. Prick lightly with a fork and chill for another half an hour. Cover the pie crust with foil and weight down with baking beans. Bake at 400°F for about 12 minutes, then remove the foil and beans, brush the base of the pastry with the reserved egg white to seal it and return to the oven for about 3–4 minutes. Remove it from the oven and lower the temperature to 375°F.

Add the sugar and maple syrup to the pumpkin purée, then the spices, salt, and bourbon. Add the eggs, one by one, beating them in well, then sift in the flour and mix lightly. Finally, add the cream and pour the filling into the pie crust. Put the pie plate on a baking sheet, transfer to the oven and bake for about 50 minutes until the filling is just set and firm, reducing the temperature to 350°F after 25 minutes.

About 10 minutes before the end of the cooking time, chop the pecan nuts finely (by hand.) Put them in a saucepan with the sugar and warm gently until the sugar starts to melt. About 5 minutes before the pie is done sprinkle the nuts evenly over the surface and return it to the oven for 5 minutes. Remove from the oven and let cool for 20 minutes before cutting. Serve lukewarm with lightly whipped cream.

ginger and cinnamon thins

It's easy enough to buy Christmas cookies, but it's worth baking them yourself if only for the gorgeous smell that permeates the kitchen. This recipe is adapted from one in an old cookery book called "Cooking for Christmas" by Shona Crawford Poole, first published in 1980.

½ cup dark brown sugar

1 stick butter, cut into cubes

6 tablespoons golden or corn syrup

6 tablespoons heavy cream

3 cups plus 2 tablespoons all-purpose flour

1 tablespoon ground ginger

1 tablespoon ground cinnamon

⅛ teaspoon ground cloves (optional)

1 teaspoon baking powder

½ teaspoon salt

2 baking sheets lined with baking parchment star-shaped cookie cutters in various sizes (or any other shapes you like, such as Christmas trees, bells etc).

Makes about 40 cookies

Sift the sugar through a coarse sieve to remove any lumps and put in a large bowl with the cubed butter. Beat together until smooth, then beat in the golden syrup and cream. Measure out the flour, add the ginger, cinnamon, cloves, baking powder, and salt and sift into another bowl. Add the flour and spice mixture to the creamed mixture a third at a time until you have a stiff dough. Form the dough into a flat disc, wrap in foil and refrigerate for at least 3 hours.

When you're ready to bake the cookies preheat the oven to 375°F. Cut off a quarter of the dough, flour your counter and rolling pin generously and roll out the dough thinly. Stamp out shapes with your cutters. Carefully lift them off the counter with a palate knife, lay them on one of the baking sheets and bake for about 8 minutes. Leave them to firm up for 2–3 minutes, then transfer to a wire rack until crisp. Repeat with the remaining pieces of dough, re-rolling the trimmings to give you as many biscuits as possible. The biscuits will keep in an airtight container for up to one week.

orange-mulled wine

If you've never made mulled wine yourself, you should try. It couldn't be simpler and tastes infinitely better than the ready-mixed versions. The only thing you have to be careful about is that the wine doesn't reach a boil.

2 bottles of medium-bodied fruity red wine

1 orange studded with cloves, plus a few orange slices to serve

thinly pared zest of ½ an unwaxed lemon

2 cinnamon sticks

6 cardamom pods, lightly crushed

a little freshly grated nutmeg or a small pinch of ground nutmeg

½ cup soft brown sugar

6 tablespoons orange-flavored liqueur, such as Cointreau or Grand Marnier, or brandy

Makes 14–16 small cups or glasses

Pour the wine into a large saucepan with 2 cups cold water. Add the orange, lemon zest, spices, and sugar and heat gently until almost at a boil. Turn down to the lowest possible heat so that the liquid barely trembles and simmer for half an hour to allow the spices to infuse thoroughly. Add

the orange-flavored liqueur then reheat gently. Strain into a large, warmed bowl and float a few thin slices of orange on top. Ladle into small cups or glasses and serve with cookies.

mulled cider

This makes such a delicious alternative to mulled wine that I'm not sure that I don't like it even better!

2 cups hard apple cider
½ cup Calvados (French apple brandy) or brandy
3 cups soft apple cider or apple juice
⅓ cup soft brown sugar
a thinly pared strip of lemon zest
2 cinnamon sticks
8 cloves
6 even-sized slices of dried apple, halved, to garnish

Makes 10–12 glasses

Put the hard cider, Calvados, and soft apple cider in a large saucepan. Add the sugar, lemon zest, cinnamon sticks, and cloves and heat very gently until the sugar has

dissolved. Heat until almost at a boil, then turn off the heat, add the halved, dried apple slices and leave the pan for half an hour for the flavors to infuse. Reheat the punch again, taking care not to bring it to a boil and serve in heatproof cups or glasses with a slice of the apple in each.

egg nog

Once you've tasted this delicious light, foamy punch, I suspect you'll want to make it every year. This version is adapted from a recipe in top American bartender Dale Degroff's "The Craft of the Cocktail."

3 very fresh large organic eggs
⅓ cup superfine sugar
6 tablespoons bourbon
6 tablespoons spiced rum
2⅓ cups whole milk
1 cup plus 2 tablespoons whipping cream
a whole nutmeg, for grating

Serves 6–8

Separate the egg yolks carefully from the whites and put them in separate large bowls. Beat the egg yolks with an electric hand-held whisk, gradually adding ¼ cup of the sugar, until they turn light in color and moussey in texture. Beat in the bourbon and spiced rum, then stir in the milk and cream.

Clean and dry your whisk thoroughly then whisk the egg whites until beginning to stiffen. Add the remaining sugar to the whites and whisk until they form a soft peak. Fold the whites into the egg nog mixture and grate over a little nutmeg.

Ladle out the egg nog into small glasses or cups. Have teaspoons available for those who prefer to spoon rather than sip it.

a Chinese New Year dinner

menu for 4

The Chinese New Year is one of those annual events that just captures the imagination. It is celebrated in such a colorful and joyous way and Chinese food is so delicious, quick and simple to make that we all feel inspired to have a go at it. This is a menu where you could easily buy in the dim sum and even the dessert (though this one is fun to make) but do have a go at the really delicious seafood stir-fry.

sesame shrimp toasts and other dim sum

TO DRINK I've discovered that a good cold gin and tonic is exceptionally refreshing with fried dim sum, such as shrimp toasts and spring rolls.

luxury seafood stir-fry

with steamed bok choy

TO DRINK There are two ways to go with the wine for Chinese food—an aromatic white such as Riesling (I would recommend a young dry one from Germany or Alsace,) or a fruity Bordeaux rosé, which works surprisingly well.

stem ginger and almond ice cream, mandarin oranges, and fortune cookies

TO DRINK Finish with a cup of delicate jasmine or chrysanthemum tea.

a selection of dim sum

Frankly, I think life is too short to make your own dim sum, so unless you're already an expert at rolling miniature spring rolls and making featherlight steamed dumplings, I would order them in from your local carryout or buy them ready-made. The exception are these simple sesame shrimp toasts, which are much easier to handle than the classic Chinese deep-fried ones and can be prepared ahead and baked at the last minute.

sesame shrimp toasts

12 oz. cooked, shelled shrimp

2–3 scallions, trimmed and finely chopped

1 teaspoon finely grated fresh ginger

1 teaspoon finely grated fresh garlic

1½ teaspoons Thai fish sauce

2 teaspoons light soy sauce

¼ teaspoon sesame oil

1 egg white

1 tablespoon ground rice

a pinch of sugar

about 5 thin slices of white bread, preferably 2–3 days old

about ½ cup sesame seeds

sea salt and freshly ground black pepper

2 non-stick baking sheets

Makes about 30 toasts

Put the shrimp in a food processor along with all the other ingredients, except the bread and sesame seeds, and whizz until smooth. Transfer to a bowl, cover, and refrigerate for an hour or 2 for the flavors to mellow.

Preheat the oven to 450°F. Cut the crusts off the bread and toast lightly. Let cool, then spread each slice thickly with the shrimp paste. Cut each slice into 6. Put the sesame seeds in a shallow bowl. Press the shrimp toasts upper-side down lightly into the sesame seeds, then lay them on the baking sheets. Bake in the preheated oven for about 5–6 minutes until the toasts are warm and the sesame seeds lightly browned. Let cool for 10 minutes before serving.

luxury seafood stir-fry

This recipe may look complicated, but it's simply a matter of assembling the ingredients and throwing them together at the last minute in a wok.

1 lb. large shrimp, thawed if frozen

7 oz. fresh queen (small) scallops

1 tablespoon cornstarch

3 tablespoons sunflower or light olive oil

4–6 scallions, trimmed and thinly sliced

4½ oz. shiitake mushrooms, wiped and thinly sliced

7 oz. broccoli, cut into small florets

1 garlic clove, crushed

1 piece of fresh ginger, about 1-inch square, peeled and grated

½ teaspoon Sichuan pepper or crushed chiles (optional)

sea salt and freshly ground white pepper

For the sauce:

1 cup vegetable stock

freshly squeezed juice of 1 large lemon (about 3–4 tablespoons)

3–4 tablespoons rice wine, sake or fino sherry

1 tablespoon superfine sugar

1 tablespoon light soy sauce (or 1½ teaspoons dark soy sauce)

1 heaping teaspoon cornstarch

a wok

Serves 4–6

Reserve any liquid from the shrimp and scallops. Pat them dry with paper towels and put in a large bowl. Sprinkle over the cornstarch, season with 1 teaspoon salt and ½ teaspoon white pepper and toss thoroughly, then cover and set aside (in the fridge if you're preparing the dish more than half an hour in advance.) Microwave or blanch the broccoli in boiling, salted water for 2 minutes. Drain and set aside.

To make the sauce, combine the stock in a measuring cup with the lemon juice and 3 tablespoons of the rice wine. Stir in the sugar and soy sauce and check the seasoning, adding more rice wine or other ingredients to taste. Mix the cornstarch with 1 tablespoon water.

When you're ready to cook, heat the wok, add the oil and tip in the scallions and mushrooms. Stir-fry for 2 minutes, then add the broccoli, garlic, and ginger. Stir-fry for another minute then season with Sichuan pepper, if using. Tip in the seafood, the sauce and any liquid from the shrimp and scallops and cook, stirring, until it comes to a boil (about 3 minutes.) Add the cornstarch mixture and stir until thickened. Remove from the heat and check the seasoning, adding extra salt or pepper if needed. Serve with steamed bok choy.

stem ginger and almond ice cream

This recipe is simplicity itself as I use store-bought vanilla ice cream as the base. Omit the fresh ginger if you prefer a milder, less spicy flavor.

6–8 pieces of stem ginger, plus 3 tablespoons of syrup from the jar

½ cup ginger beer (such as Reed's) or ginger wine (such as Stone's)

1–2 teaspoons fresh ginger, finely grated (optional)

1 tablespoon orange-flavored liqueur, such as Cointreau, plus extra to serve

1–2 drops of pure almond extract, to taste

1 pint premium vanilla ice cream

fortune cookies and canned mandarin oranges, to serve

Serves 4

Chop the stem ginger very finely and put it in a small bowl. In a small saucepan, combine the ginger syrup, ginger beer, fresh ginger (is using), and orange liqueur. Bring to a boil and let simmer for about 8 minutes until the mixture has reduced by half. Strain into the bowl with the pieces of stem ginger. Add a drop of 2 of almond extract to taste. Let cool for 15 minutes.

Remove the ice cream from the freeze to soften, but don't let it melt. Put the softened ice cream in a large bowl. Using a rubber spatula, swirl the cooled ginger syrup mixture through the ice cream until well combined. Spoon the flavored ice cream into a shallow freezerproof container and return it to the freezer to firm up again. About 30 minutes before serving, transfer the ice cream to the fridge to make it easier to scoop.

Serve with fortune cookies, or another light crisp cookies, and mandarin oranges, drained and marinated in orange-flavored liqueur. Do give each person 8 segments—8 is a sacred number in China and considered to bring luck and prosperity!

tea in China

Tea is so much a part of life in China that it is drunk at almost any time of day—though rarely with meals. For the most part it is "green" or unfermented tea, sometimes served on its own, sometimes infused with jasmine petals. There is a delightful ritual to the whole preparation and consumption that is repetitive and soothing. It's well worth seeking out fine teas, many of which can now be bought on-line, and acquiring delicate porcelain bowls in which to serve them. The temperature and source of the water is also critical to the flavor and leaves should not be steeped for too long a time.

a quick deli meal

menu for 4

Sometimes you want to have friends over in the middle of the week. Most times you don't have time to cook. Solution? A visit to your local store's deli counter, where you can easily source the groceries for this simple, throw-it-together menu. All you have to do on the night is make a creamy mushroom risotto, which you can stir while you chat to your friends in the kitchen. My cocktail desserts are also a boon when you're pressed for time as they are simple, glamorous, and fun.

❧

antipasti

wild mushroom risotto
with arugula salad

lemon and raspberry iced vodka Martinis
choc-mint Martinis
banoffee Martinis

TO DRINK Italian wines are the instinctive choice with this largely Italian-inspired menu. A dry Italian white such as a Pinot Grigio would go perfectly well with both the antipasti and the risotto. Try one from the Alto Adige in the north-east of Italy, which produces some of the best the country has to offer. Alternatively, you could switch to a supple, medium-bodied Italian red with the main course: something like a Chianti or Rosso di Montepulciano.

antipasti

Make a colorful spread of Italian cured meats and cheeses and roasted or grilled vegetables. Take your pick from Parma ham, two different types of salami (the kind with fennel seeds is particularly delicious,) mini mozzarella balls, or a buffalo mozzarella and cherry tomato salad (buy some extra fresh basil to garnish,) roasted bell peppers, zucchini, and eggplant, grilled artichokes and marinated mushrooms. Serve with a selection of ciabatta and breadsticks.

wild mushroom risotto

Risottos always go down well and, once you've got the hang of them, they are incredibly easy to make. Use wild mushrooms in season or cremini mushrooms with some dried porcini when they're not available.

7 oz. wild mushrooms or 9 oz. cremini mushrooms and 1 oz. dried porcini, soaked for 15 minutes in warm water

2 tablespoons light olive oil

6 tablespoons unsalted butter

1 small–medium onion, finely chopped

1½ cups arborio or carnaroli risotto rice

5 cups fresh chicken stock or stock made with vegetable bouillon powder

½ cup dry white wine

3 heaping tablespoons Parmesan cheese, plus extra to serve

salt and freshly ground black pepper

Serves 4

Clean the fresh mushrooms by lightly brushing or wiping them with a damp cloth. Slice them thinly. If you're using porcini drain them and slice them too. Heat a medium skillet, add 1 tablespoon of oil and

3 tablespoons of the butter and briefly fry the fresh mushrooms until lightly browned. Heat the remaining oil and 1½ tablespoons of the remaining butter in a large saucepan then add the onion. Stir and cook over a medium heat, for about 3 minutes, then tip in the rice and stir. Let it cook for about 3 minutes without coloring, stirring occasionally so that it doesn't catch on the pan. Meanwhile, heat the stock in another saucepan until it is almost at a boil and leave over low heat. Pour the wine into the rice. It will sizzle and evaporate almost immediately. Add the dried mushrooms, if using, then gradually add the stock, a ladleful at a time, stirring the risotto in between and cooking it until the liquid has almost been absorbed. Then add the next lot of stock and repeat until the rice is nice and creamy but still has a little "bite" to it. This will take about 20 minutes. About 5 minutes before the end of the cooking time, stir in the sautéed mushrooms, leaving a few for garnishing. When the risotto is ready, stir in the remaining butter and the Parmesan and season to taste with salt and pepper. Leave the pan covered for a few minutes while you reheat the remaining mushrooms. Serve the risotto in bowls topped with a few mushrooms and some extra Parmesan. Serve with a small handful of arugula.

Take both the sorbets out of the freezer 20 minutes before you want to serve them and transfer to the fridge. Scoop a couple of balls of sorbet into each glass (same flavor or mixed) and pour over a splash of vodka.

* Vodka won't actually freeze but keep it in the freezer and it will be wonderfully cold.

choc-mint Martinis

4 scoops chocolate mint ice cream
4 shots chilled or frozen vodka*
2 shots coffee-flavored liqueur, such as Kahlúa
cocoa mix, to garnish

4 Martini glasses, frosted in the freezer

Makes 4 drinks

Put the ice cream in a blender with the vodka and coffee-flavored liqueur. Whizz until smooth then try the blend, adjusting the proportions of ice cream, vodka, or liqueur to taste. Pour into the glasses and sift a little cocoa mix over the surface.

banoffee Martinis

1 ripe banana, sliced
ice cubes
3 shots vanilla-flavored vodka or ordinary vodka and a few drops of pure vanilla extract
2 shots toffee- or caramel-flavored liqueur
2 shots milk
a small pinch of ground nutmeg (optional)
cocoa mix, to garnish

2 Martini glasses, frosted in the freezer

Makes 2 drinks

Whizz the banana in a blender with the vodka. Tip the purée into a shaker full of ice cubes. Add the toffee liqueur, milk, and nutmeg, if using, and shake vigorously. Strain into the glasses and sift a little cocoa mix over the surface.

dessert cocktails

Easy, light, stunning. Iced vodka Martinis are the perfect midweek dessert, so long as you don't have too many of them! Ultra-sweet, creamy cocktails also make a brilliant instant dessert, so try these too.

lemon and raspberry iced vodka Martinis

1 pint lemon sorbet
1 pint raspberry sorbet
1 pint frozen* vodka

4 Martini glasses, frosted in the freezer

Makes 4 drinks

a fine wine dinner

menu for 6

Sometimes the starting point for a menu is a bottle—or bottles—of special wine. You may feel you have to pull all the culinary stops out—but don't! Nothing suits fine wines better than simple food. A clean-flavored seafood appetizer, a prime cut of meat, an elegant, classic dessert—there's nothing in this meal that's too complicated or that could clash with a treasured bottle. Let the wine be the hero for once...

potted shrimp

TO DRINK Potted shrimp is an astonishingly good match for good white Burgundy or other mature Chardonnay, so I would kick off with that.

roast fillet of beef with soy and butter sauce

roast new potatoes with garlic and rosemary

TO DRINK The gentle flavors of the meat sauce won't overwhelm an older red wine, so this is the occasion to bring out an aged bottle of Bordeaux, Burgundy, Barolo, or a Rioja Gran Reserva that you have been saving for a special occasion.

roast pears with sweet wine, honey, and pine nuts

TO DRINK The perfect excuse to crack open a bottle of Sauternes. Serve it well chilled in small glasses.

chocolates, coffee, and cognac

roast pears with sweet wine, honey, and pine nuts

Roasting pears in wine transforms them from everyday fruit into a light but luxurious dessert. The trick is to use an inexpensive wine for cooking and a better wine of the same type to serve with it.

freshly squeezed juice of 1 lemon (about 3 tablespoons)

9 just-ripe, small pears

3 tablespoons butter, softened

3 tablespoons fragrant honey

²/₃ cup Premières Côtes de Bordeaux or late-harvested Sauvignon or Semillon

¹/₃ cup pine nuts

2 teaspoons sugar

¼ cup heavy cream

2 teaspoons vanilla sugar or ½ teaspoon pure vanilla extract and 2 teaspoons sugar

a large roasting pan or ovenproof dish (big enough to take the pears in a single layer,) well buttered

Serves 6

Preheat the oven to 375°F. Strain the lemon juice into a small bowl. Cut each pear in half, peel it and cut away the core. Dip it in the lemon juice to stop it discoloring. Place it cut-side upwards in the roasting pan or dish. Arrange the pears so that they fit snugly in one layer. Put a knob of butter in the centre of each half. Drizzle the pears with the honey and pour over the leftover lemon juice and the wine.

Bake in the preheated oven for about 50 minutes–1 hour, turning the pears halfway through. If the pears produce a lot of juice turn the heat up to 400°F to concentrate the juices and form a syrup. Remove from the

oven and let cool for about 20 minutes. (You can part-cook the dish for about 30 minutes a couple of hours before dinner, then finish cooking it once you sit down at table, allowing it to cool during the entrée.)

Meanwhile, toast the pine nuts lightly in a skillet, shaking them occasionally until they start to brown. Sprinkle over the sugar and continue to cook until the sugar melts and caramelizes. Sweeten the cream with the vanilla sugar and heat until lukewarm. Arrange 3 pear halves on each plate, trickle over about a tablespoon of warmed cream and scatter over the pine nuts.

chocolates, coffee, and cognac

For a special occasion, you can serve this at the
end of the meal, otherwise it makes a great
substitute for a dessert. Source the best hand-made
chocolates you can find, preferably made from
bittersweet chocolate, including some truffles for
contrast. Brew up some real coffee—espresso for
those who want it and an Americano for those who
prefer a less intense brew—and serve with the best
cognac or Spanish brandy you can afford.

seasonal cheeseboards

Wine and cheese is supposed to be the perfect match, but how often have you been disappointed at the combination? Your favorite red wine may taste great with one or two of the cheeses on the board, but clash horribly with another. Or a delicate cheese may be totally overwhelmed by the wine. It's time we changed the way we think about cheeseboards, designing them, like other foods we serve, to reflect the seasons and our mood. It's an approach that makes abundant sense, as so many cheeses themselves are seasonal. Why serve the same cheeseboard in Spring as you do in Fall?

It also helps to limit the number of cheeses you serve and pick them carefully. If you include a strong, stinky French cheese and a pungent blue in your selection, for example, you'll struggle to find a wine to go with them both. The traditional approach is to serve the widest range of cheeses you can afford, displaying your generosity as a host, but the chances are that your guests will enjoy the experience just as much if you select two or three that work perfectly together.

You can also be a bit more imaginative about the way you dress your cheeseboard, introducing accompaniments that will complement the flavor of your cheeses and reflect the time of year. Warm, rich dried fruits, for example, in winter when fresh fruits are less widely available; fresh salad greens in spring. Finally, don't get too struck on the idea that the only accompaniment for a cheeseboard is a glass of red wine. There are many other drinks that work just as well. Crisp white wines in spring, for example, or a glass of sweet sherry or Madeira rather than port. It's sometimes a great deal easier to find a Belgian beer to match a powerful cheese than a wine and artisanal cider can also be a great pairing.

spring

Spring and early summer is the ideal time of year to enjoy fresh young goat cheeses and their perfect partner Sauvignon Blanc. Choose two or three cheeses for contrast: one young, light and moussey, one that has been matured a little longer and one that has been rolled in herbs. Serve them with a lightly dressed herb salad bought from the farmers' market. You could also add a wedge of tangy, fresh Italian pecorino, and a few shelled fava beans, a delicious combination. Breads should be light too—slices of ciabatta and some crisp Italian flatbread such as *carta di musica*. My preferred choice of Sauvignon would be a minerally Sancerre or Pouilly Fumé, but choose any unoaked Sauvignon that you enjoy.

summer

Now the flavors are richer and fuller, begging for a full-bodied red wine. The type of cheese that works best are the smooth, tangy hard sheeps' milk cheeses you traditionally find in Spain and the Basque region of France, full-flavored but without any touch of bitterness. I also like to add a Fleur de Maquis, a Corsican cheese rolled in rosemary and fennel. Add some other Mediterranean ingredients—a few chewy sun-dried tomatoes, some olives and olive bread—and you've got the perfect foil for a rich southern French red from the Languedoc or the Rhône, or a Spanish red like a Rioja.

fall

The ploughman's lunch re-invented. Forget wine for once and turn to cider, the natural accompaniment for autumn fruits and flavors. Mix and match among ancient and modern British and Irish cheeses—a fine cheddar, an Irish Adrahan, or other washed-rind cheese, a snowy white-rinded Tunworth, maybe even a mellow blue. Serve with fine, flavorful eating apples and pears, a mild apple chutney (homemade or store-bought) and an old-fashioned white crusty loaf, and pour chunky glasses of cool, artisanal cider, offering your guests a choice of dry or medium-dry if you wish. You could even offer brandy glasses of Somerset Cider Brandy or Calvados to round off the meal.

winter

Port and blue cheese is a classic pairing, but give it a modern twist. Serve three contrasting cheeses, say a Stilton, a Roquefort and a mild Gorgonzola, or Harbourne Blue (a mild blue goat cheese from Devon in England) and serve them with a top class collection of dried fruits such as Medjool dates, figs, or raisins, and a handful of walnuts and Brazil nuts. Echo the dried fruit flavors with my simple raisin and rosemary bread (see opposite) or a walnut bread, and introduce a little crunch with a few handcut oatcakes. This is the perfect occasion to bring out a vintage port (which you'll need to decant) or serve a fine Sauternes or a Tokay from Hungary. What blue cheeses need is sweetness.

Vivid orange Mimolette served with Medjool dates, dried apricots, and figs makes a perfect winter cheese plate. Serve with a hearty red wine such as a Syrah or Shiraz.

raisin and rosemary bread

A quick, simple bread that's perfect with cheese.

2 cups bread flour

1 cup plus 2 tablespoons whole-wheat flour

¾ cup rye flour

1½ teaspoons easy-blend or quick-acting yeast

1½ teaspoons fine sea salt

1 tablespoon finely chopped rosemary, plus 2 extra sprigs for topping

1 tablespoon dark brown sugar

1⅓ cups tepid water

2 tablespoons olive oil

⅔ cup raisins

a baking sheet, lightly oiled

Makes 1 large loaf

Mix together the bread, whole-wheat, and rye flours in a large bowl. Mix in the yeast, salt, and chopped rosemary. Dissolve the sugar in 2 tablespoons of the water. Make a well in the middle of the flour and pour in the dissolved sugar and olive oil, followed by the rest of the water. Start working the flour into the liquid with a wooden spoon, then mix with your hands until all the flour is incorporated. Turn the dough onto a floured board and knead for 5 minutes or until the dough begins to feel elastic. Flatten the dough and add half the raisins. Fold over and knead for a couple of seconds, then repeat with the remaining raisins. Carry on kneading for another 5 minutes until smooth. Place the dough in a large bowl covered with a lightly dampened kitchen towel and leave for about 45–50 minutes until doubled in size. Tip the dough out of the bowl and press down on it to knock out the air. Roll up the dough into a long sausage shape, tucking in the ends. Place on the baking sheet, make 3–4 diagonal cuts in the dough with a sharp knife, cover with the kitchen towel and leave for another 25 minutes. Meanwhile, preheat the oven to 400°F. Brush the top of the loaf lightly with water and scatter over the leaves from the rosemary sprigs, pressing them lightly into the dough. Bake for about 35–40 minutes until the loaf is well browned and sounds hollow when you tap it on the base. Cool on a wire rack for a good 45 minutes before serving.

just desserts

An alternative to inviting people over for a meal or drinks and snacks, is to just invite them over for something sweet. It could be simply to join you for dessert, or for a nightcap and a sweet nibble. Or you could host an old-fashioned coffee morning (see page 142)—whatever happened to that tradition? Or why not host an indulgent Chocolate Evening—see page 145 for plenty of ideas. There are so many ways to play this...

You could offer a selection of petit fours or dessert tapas (see page 71)—little cakes and tartlets, colourful macaroons or meringues, homemade mini florentines (opposite), served with some different sweet wines to try. I find liqueurs are frequently better than wines with chocolate desserts. Think of the flavors you find in a box of liqueur chocolates—cherry, apricot, orange, blackcurrant, mint, coffee, hazelnut, almond, and you can find an equivalent liqueur (cherry or apricot brandy, Grand Marnier, cassis, crème de menthe, Kahlùa, Frangelico, and Disaronno, for example.) Most taste best lightly chilled; some, like cherry brandy, are good frozen. Serve them in shot glasses or antique liqueur glasses and your friends will be truly impressed.

cranberry and cherry florentines

These have to be the easiest cookies in the world, but they look sensationally impressive.

6 tablespoons butter
½ cup sugar
2 teaspoons fragrant honey
½ cup blanched almonds
⅔ cup mixed sun-dried cranberries, cherries, and blueberries
¾ cup all-purpose flour
4½ oz. premium bittersweet chocolate (minimum 70% cocoa solids)
2–3 non-stick baking sheets or baking sheets lined with baking parchment or foil

Makes 20–24 biscuits

Preheat the oven to 350°F. Put the butter, sugar, and honey in a saucepan and melt over low heat. When the sugar has dissolved, bring almost to a boil, then take the pan off the stove. Stir in the almonds and fruit, then tip in the flour and mix thoroughly. Spoon heaping teaspoonfuls of the mixture onto the baking sheets, leaving plenty of space between each blob. Flatten them slightly with the back of your spoon so that they cook evenly and bake for 10–12 minutes until the florentines have spread and are turning brown at the edges. Take them out of the oven, cool for about 3 minutes, then carefully lift them off the baking sheets and transfer them to a wire rack. When they are completely cold, break the chocolate into squares, place it in a medium heatproof bowl and melt in the microwave or over a pan of barely simmering water, taking care that the bowl doesn't touch the water. Lay the cookies flat-side upwards on a sheet of waxed paper and brush or spread the chocolate over them with a pastry brush or a flat-bladed knife. Leave them out until the chocolate sets, then store in an airtight container until ready to serve.

coffee and cake

How about postponing the weekend shopping and chores and inviting friends round for an indulgent Saturday morning get-together? Buy in your cakes by all means, or try one of these two irresistible recipes and the smell of freshly baked cakes will greet your guests.

Adjust the strength of your coffee to the cake you're serving. A strong dark espresso or Americano, for example, is ideal for a dark chocolate or rich Sticky Toffee Pudding Cake, while a lighter sponge cake will taste better with a more fragrant, refreshing breakfast coffee. Cappuccinos are delicious with lighter chocolate and coffee-flavored cakes.

Malibu, lime, and coconut cake

Even if you're not a fan of Malibu, I promise you you'll love this exotic coconut-flavored cake. If you are, you'll be in seventh heaven!

1½ sticks unsalted butter, at room temperature, diced

1½ cups superfine sugar

3 large eggs

1½ cups self-rising flour

2 tablespoons coconut milk flour

½ teaspoon baking powder

3 tablespoons Malibu (coconut-flavored liqueur)

a little grated lime zest

¾ cup confectioners' sugar, sifted twice

1–1½ tablespoons freshly squeezed lime juice

3 tablespoons toasted coconut flakes

a lightly greased 2 lb. loaf pan lined with a strip of baking parchment

Serves 8–10

Preheat the oven to 325°F. Put the butter in a large bowl with the sugar and beat with an electric hand-held whisk or a wooden spoon until light and fluffy. Lightly beat one of the eggs and add it to the mixture with a tablespoon of the flour that has been sifted along with the coconut milk flour and baking powder. Beat in well and repeat with the remaining eggs, adding a spoonful of flour with each addition. Mix in the Malibu, then add the remaining flour and coconut flour, mixing in lightly and quickly. Spoon into the prepared loaf pan and spread the top evenly. Bake in the preheated oven for 45–50 minutes until the cake is well risen and firm and slightly shrunken away from the sides. Remove the pan from the oven and cool for 10 minutes, then turn the cake out of the pan and leave to cool on a wire rack. Mix the lime zest with the sifted confectioners' sugar and add just enough lime juice to make a thick but still spreadable consistency. Spread or pour over the top of the cake and sprinkle over the toasted coconut flakes.

This is delicious served with a French-style café crème—a white coffee with a little bit of froth, but not quite as frothy as an Italian cappuccino.

sticky toffee pudding cake

¾ cup dried dates, chopped

1 teaspoon baking soda

1 cup moderately strong hot black coffee (e.g. from a French press)

1 cup plus 2 tablespoons all-purpose flour

3 tablespoons butter, chilled and cubed

⅓ cup walnuts, finely chopped

1 cup superfine sugar

1 teaspoon baking powder

½ teaspoon fine sea salt

½ teaspoon pure vanilla extract

1 large egg

For the topping:

⅓ cup walnuts, finely chopped

1 teaspoon raw granulated sugar

2 tablespoons unsalted butter

¼ cup light brown sugar

4 tablespoons whipping cream

a rectangular, non-stick baking pan 12 x 8 inches, lightly greased

Makes 15 squares

Preheat the oven to 350°F. Put the dates in a bowl, add the baking soda, and pour over the hot coffee. Put the flour in another bowl, tip in the cubed butter and use your fingertips to rub it in until it resembles coarse breadcrumbs.

Add the chopped walnuts to the flour mixture with the superfine sugar, baking powder, and salt. Beat the egg with the vanilla extract and add to the date mixture then tip the date mixture, into the dry ingredients and beat well. Turn the mixture into the prepared baking pan. Bake in the preheated oven for about 35–40 minutes or until well risen and firm to the touch. Remove from the oven and let cool for 10 minutes while you make the topping.

Heat the walnuts in a saucepan with the granulated sugar, shaking them occasionally until they are lightly toasted. Combine the butter in a small saucepan with the brown sugar and cream. Heat over low heat, stirring until the sugar has dissolved, then bring to a boil. Pour evenly over the cake, smoothing over the icing with a knife, then scatter the toasted walnuts on top. When the cake is completely cool, cut it into squares and carefully remove from the pan using a cake slice or palate knife.

This is particularly good served with freshly brewed black coffee.

a chocolate evening

No-one—even if they're on a diet—is going to refuse an invitation to come over for a chocolate evening (if they hesitate, just tell them they don't need to eat the next day...). There are so many ways to play it. You could serve a variety of different chocolate desserts such as some individual mousses or chocolate pots, a chocolate cake, and a chocolate tart such as the one opposite, one of my all-time favorite recipes.

Alternatively, you could serve a selection of different chocolate cakes and cookies—some chocolate muffins and warm chocolate chip cookies perhaps. You could even have friends over for an indulgent chocolate fondue, offering fruits such as strawberries, apricots, and pieces of banana for dunking into the molten chocolate.

You could base the event—although this would be more of a morning than an evening occasion —on hot chocolate and serve baskets of Danish pastries or some French pâtisserie, such as pain au chocolat. Or just keep it simple and invite friends round for chocolate and Cognac after dinner (see page 135.)

If your event is a success you could start a local chocolate club, meeting with friends once a month for different chocolate-themed evenings and trying new chocolate recipes from around the world?

hazelnut, chocolate, and cardamom cream pie

For the pie crust:

5 tablespoons unsalted butter, softened

3 tablespoons confectioners' sugar

3 tablespoons hazelnuts

1 cup all-purpose flour, unsifted

1 egg yolk

For the filling:

10 green cardamom pods

1¼ cups heavy cream

7 oz. premium bittersweet chocolate (minimum 70% cocoa solids), broken into chunks

2 tablespoons unsalted butter

1 tablespoon unsweetened cocoa powder, sifted, to decorate

a baking sheet
a 9-inch fluted pie plate

Serves 8

Preheat the oven to 375°F. Spread the hazelnuts out on a baking sheet and toast in the preheated oven for 15 minutes or until lightly browned. Cool, then chop in a food processor or coffee grinder (you may have to do this in batches.) Cream the butter with the sifted confectioners' sugar, add 3 tablespoons of the hazelnuts then gradually work in the flour. Beat the egg yolk with 1 tablespoon water and add to the mixture, gradually pulling it into a ball.

Turn out onto a floured board or counter and roll or press it out gently into a round slightly smaller than the pie plate. Carefully lower it into the plate (don't worry if it breaks) and press it round and up the side until you have formed a pie crust. Chill in the fridge for at least half an hour, then prick the base and bake it in the oven for about 15–20 minutes until lightly browned. Let cool.

Meanwhile, crush the cardamom pods with in a mortar with a pestle or with the end of a rolling pin. Remove the green husks and finely grind the seeds. Add to the cream and gently warm in a saucepan until the surface is just beginning to tremble. (Don't let it reach a boil.) Take off the heat and add the chocolate chunks, butter and the remaining ground hazelnuts. Set aside to cool, but don't let it get cold. Pour into the pie crust and put in the fridge for at least 2 hours. Dust the surface with cocoa powder before serving.

This is delicious with a glass of Frangelico (Italian hazelnut liqueur.)

the art of party planning

It's easy to lose sight of the main reason for having a party: to enjoy yourself and to make sure your guests have a good time. All too often your worries about what food to serve and whether your guests will get on becomes such an overriding concern or you spend so much time slaving away in the kitchen that you end up completely stressed and worn out. The good news, though, is that it's never been easier to throw a party without spending hours cooking or spending a fortune on caterers. You can literally buy in everything you need—canapés, platters of cold meats or seafood, hot dishes, vegetables, salads, cheeseboards, and gorgeous, gooey desserts—which completely takes the terror out of entertaining. If you tell yourself that you don't have to cook a thing if you don't want to, you can then concentrate on the dishes you do best or most enjoy making. What you do need to do is to focus on what sort of party you want, so ask yourself the following questions:

WHAT SORT OF PARTY IS IT?

Do you want to celebrate something special or simply to get a few friends together? Do you want it to be an occasion that everyone will remember or just a relaxed affair? Are you happy for it to last for hours or do you just want to "pay your dues" with a pop-in-when-you-like drinks party for neighbours or colleagues at work?

CAN YOU PULL IT OFF?

Have you got the space to invite as many people as you want? Or the equipment (see page 148)? Can you throw the sort of party you have in mind on your budget? Do you have the time—or the skill—to prepare the sort of meal you're planning? For example, if you've never cooked for more than four friends before, you might find cooking for 20 daunting without help. If so, how are you going to get around that? Get professional help? Buy in prepared dishes? Enlist help from family and friends? If you're going to make part of the food yourself, don't leave yourself too many things that require last-minute attention or embark on recipes that you've never attempted before.

THE MENU

There are plenty of menus in the book that can be adapted for a crowd—just remember when you're scaling up recipes for larger numbers that not every ingredient needs to be doubled or tripled. Go easy on spices and other seasonings, tasting before you add more.

Quantities will vary depending on the age and sex of your guests (younger guests and men tending to eat more than older guests and women,) but as a general rule I would allow six to eight canapés or nibbles per person for a drinks party, of which one or two could be sweet, and one and a half servings in total of any entrée, two servings of salad or vegetables and two of dessert, on the assumption that a third to a half of your guests will come back for a second helping. If you want to limit the amount that your guests eat, don't offer too many options, as people like to try everything, especially desserts!

Remember to check if there is anything your guests can't eat. Food intolerances are quite common these days, so it's wise to have at least one option that is vegetarian, wheat- and dairy-free (rice-based dishes are particularly useful in this respect).

THE DRINKS

Again, the more different types of drink you offer, the more your guests will drink and the more glasses they'll use. A choice of two types of wine, two different soft drinks and water is plenty, although you can obviously lay on one or two beers and by-the-pitcher drinks (much easier than making individual cocktails) if you wish.

A reasonable amount to cater for is half a bottle of wine per head, although if a party is due to go on for quite a time or you have guests who are likely to drink rather more than that, allow a bottle each in total.

Good choices for a drinks party are Champagne or sparkling wine or a light, refreshing white and a soft, fruity red. (Avoid wines that are heavily oaked or high in alcohol, which can easily result in your guests drinking more than they realize and can also make them uncomfortably hot and flushed.) As a general rule, you'll probably need twice as much white wine as red.

For an event with hot food, you need wines with a little more weight—consult my food and wine matching guidelines overleaf for the individual dishes you're planning to serve. Either way, it's best to go for wines that everyone will enjoy and that are not too hard on the pocket. When I'm catering for large numbers, I tend to go for easy crowd-pleasers rather than more esoteric wines—lighter styles of Chardonnay and Sauvignon Blanc for the whites and soft reads such as Merlot or Pinot Noir for the reds. If you're holding an outdoor event like a barbecue, you could easily serve rosé instead of a white, so popular has it become. Pink fizz is also great fun too, especially for a summer tea party (see page 56).

Finally, avoid the temptation to buy a case of cheap wine that you haven't tried before just because it's on special offer. Often stores discount wines that have reached the end of their shelf-life, so you may end up with a batch that's tasting rather flat and tired. If at all possible, try a bottle before you buy in bulk.

THE EQUIPMENT

It's rare to have enough glasses, flatware, and cutlery to cater for a crowd, so make sure you hire or borrow enough for everyone. Many wine shops and supermarkets now offer glass hire—play safe and allow two wine glasses per head.

You also need plenty of ice and large buckets or bins to keep wine and beer cool. (Water and ice used together is more effective than ice alone.)

If you're organizing a barbecue or any other event that requires special equipment (such as blenders or juicers for a juice bar—see page 19,) again, make sure you have a sufficient number to avoid long delays in producing the food or drinks.

matching wine to food

Finding a precise match for a dish can be tricky because there are so many variables: how it is cooked, whether there are any strong spice or herbal accents, how many other ingredients there are on the plate. So, to make it as easy as possible, I've concentrated on the style of food here rather than individual dishes, but giving specific examples where appropriate. If you don't find what you're looking for here, do look it up on my website: www.matchingfoodandwine.com

SOUPS

You don't always need wine with a soup, as one liquid doesn't really need another. The thicker the soup, the easier it is to match.

Thin soups e.g. consommés, spicy South-East Asian broths are better without wine, although dry sherry will go with a traditional consommé.

Smooth creamy soups e.g. light vegetable soups: go for a smooth, dry, unoaked white such as Chablis or Soave.

Chunky soups should be treated as you would a stew—they can take a medium-bodied white or a red wine such as a Côtes du Rhône.

APPETIZERS

Given that they're served at the beginning of a meal, a crisp, dry white, aromatic white or rosé is generally most appropriate. Sometimes a light red can work too.

Cold, fish-based dishes such as shrimp or crab salads or terrines: a crisp, dry white such as Sancerre or other Loire Sauvignon Blanc, or a Riesling (particularly good with smoked fish.) Chablis is the classic match for oysters.

Hot, fish-based appetizers e.g fish cakes or scallops: Chardonnay is usually a safe bet except with spicy flavors when unoaked, fruity or aromatic whites work better.

Charcuterie (saucisson, salami, pâtés, and air-dried hams): dry rosé and light reds like Beaujolais.

Meat-based salads made with duck or with chicken livers: Pinot Noir.

Cheese-based appetizers with salads and cold quiches try unoaked Chardonnay, while goat cheese works well with Sauvignon Blanc. Champagne or sparkling wine pairs well with deep-fried cheese appetizers.

Vegetable-based appetizers e.g. terrines: follow similar recommendations to cold fish-based appetizers opposite. (Asparagus works well with Sauvignon Blanc).

Tapas: chilled fino or manzanilla sherry (see page 66.)

PASTA, PIZZA, AND NOODLES

It's not the type of pasta you use that determines your choice of wine, it's the sauce you put with it.

Creamy sauces e.g. spaghetti carbonara: smooth, dry, Italian unoaked whites such as Soave and Pinot Bianco.

Seafood-based sauces: crisp, dry Italian whites and citrussy Sauvignon Blancs.

Tomato-based sauces: fresh tomato sauces—crisp, dry whites such as Pinot Grigio or Sauvignon Blanc: cooked tomato sauces—a light Italian red such as Chianti or a Barbera.

Cheese-based sauces: crisp, dry, intensely flavored whites—good Pinot Grigio or

a modern Sardinian white.

Rich meat or eggplant-based sauces e.g. Bolognese: a fruity Italian red such as a Barbera or a Sangiovese, or a southern Italian or Sicilian red.

Baked pasta dishes e.g. meat lasagne: a good Chianti.

Pizza: generally, I think fruity Italian reds work better than whites, except with seafood pizzas.

Noodles: generally spicy, so crisp fruity whites or aromatic whites such as Riesling tend to work best.

RICE

Rice dishes work in a similar way to pasta with wine.

Risotto: Most light vegetable- and seafood-based risottos pair well with crisp, dry whites such as good-quality Pinot Grigio or Soave and with sparkling wines like Champagne. Richer risottos based on dried mushrooms (porcini) or beet can take a red (Pinot Noir and Dolcetto respectively.)

Spicy rice (e.g. paella, jambalaya): dry southern French or Spanish rosé and tempranillo-based reds such as those from Rioja and Navarra.

Sushi: Muscadet or dry Champagne, especially Blanc de Blancs.

FISH

Cooked simply, fish is quite delicate, but more robust cooking techniques and saucing can call for more powerful wines.

Raw fish e.g. sushi, sashimi: see notes for Sushi, above.

Pickled fish e.g. herring: lager, especially

pilsener, works better than wine.

Oily fish e.g. mackerel, sardines: sharp, lemony whites such as Rueda and modern Greek whites.

Smoked fish: dry Riesling or Spanish manzanilla sherry.

Salmon: served cold—unoaked Chardonnay e.g. Chablis; served hot in a pie or with pastry—lightly-oaked Chardonnay; with a hot butter sauce—a richer Chardonnay; seared or marinated with a spicy crust— a light red such as Pinot Noir.

Tuna: served cold in salad—Sauvignon Blanc or dry rosé; seared or grilled, a chilled Pinot Noir.

Fish in a creamy sauce including fish pie: lightly oaked Chardonnay, Chenin Blanc, or oaked white Bordeaux.

Pan-fried or broiled fish: If simply prepared this is an occasion to drink good white Burgundy or other top-quality Chardonnay or a clean-flavored white like Albariño.

Fish and fries and other fried fish: crisp, dry whites such as Sauvignon Blanc or a sparkling wine.

Seared, roasted, or grilled fish: can often take a light red, such as Pinot Noir, especially if wrapped in pancetta or served with lentils or beans.

BIRDS AND GAME

Chicken

Being a neutrally flavored bird, you need to focus more on the way chicken is cooked and the sauce that accompanies it than the chicken itself (see page 9–11.) See also recommendations for pasta sauces (opposite) and spicy food (page 152.)

Roast chicken: Good white or red Burgundy or quality New World Chardonnay or Pinot Noir; softer, riper styles of Bordeaux e.g. Pomerol and Merlot.

Broiled or char-grilled chicken: Will depend on the baste or the marinade— lighter, citrussy, herbal flavors suggest a crisp, fruity white like a Sauvignon Blanc; a spicier, sweeter marinade would work better with a jammy red like a Shiraz.

With tomatoes, peppers, and olives: a fruity, Italian red or other Sangiovese.

Coq au vin and other red wine sauces: a similar red wine to the one you use to make the dish (a robust Rhône or Languedoc red or a Syrah, I suggest.)

Fried chicken: unoaked or lightly oaked Chardonnay.

Sweet and sour or fruity sauces: Fruity Australian whites such as Semillon, Semillon-Chardonnay or Colombard, or ripe, fruity reds such as Merlot.

Chicken salads: depends a bit on the dressing. An unoaked Chardonnay or a fruity rosé will cover most eventualities but if there's a South-East Asian twist to the recipe, a Sauvignon Blanc, Riesling, Verdelho, or Viognier is likely to work much better.

Turkey

See chicken, but bear in mind that on festive occasions a roast turkey is likely to be accompanied by a flavorsome stuffing, fruity cranberry sauce, and richly-flavored vegetables such as butternut squash, which call for a more full-bodied red than a plain roast chicken: something like a fruity Pinot Noir, Shiraz or even Châteauneuf-du-Pape.

Duck

Pinot Noir almost always works except with duck confit, which is better with darker, more full-bodied southern French or Spanish red.

MEAT

Pork

Very similar in flavor to chicken, but the extra fattiness calls for wines with a little more acidity. *See also the sauces listed under Chicken, Pasta, and Spicy Food.*

Roast pork: If flavored Italian-style with garlic and fennel, choose a dry Italian white. Otherwise try a soft, fruity red such as a Pinot Noir, Merlot, or a good cru Beaujolais. Chenin Blanc and Riesling are good with cold roast pork.

Pork with apples and cider: hard cider is better than wine.

Sausages: robust, fruity southern French or Spanish red.

Hot gammon: a fruity red such as Merlot or a Carmenère.

Cold ham: Chablis or other unoaked Chardonnay and Beaujolais.

See also Charcuterie under Appetizers.

Lamb

Roast or broiled lamb: a good partner for a serious red, particularly red Bordeaux and other Cabernet- and Merlot-based wines, Rioja and Chianti Classico.

Lamb shanks and casseroles: robust, rustic reds such as those from the Rhône, Southern France, and Spain.

Greek-style lamb kebabs with mint and lemon: can be partnered with a fruity red but equally good with a citrussy white.

Lamb tagines: Rioja Reserva or soft, pruney southern Italian reds. *See also Spicy Foods.*

Beef and venison

Roasts and steaks: any fine red you enjoy. Argentinian Malbec is a particularly good steak wine.

Casseroles, stews, and pies: can cover quite a wide range of flavors from a beef stew with dumplings (for which beer is a better accompaniment than wine) to a rich oxtail stew (try Zinfandel.) A useful guide is that if you use wine to make the stew, drink a robust red; if you use beer, drink ale.

Teriyaki or stir-fried beef: a ripe fruity red such as a Chilean or Australian Cabernet Sauvignon or a full-bodied New World Pinot Noir. *See also Spicy Foods.*

Veal

For many dishes my recommendations would be similar to those for pork although given the cost of veal, you might feel justified in indulging in a rather better bottle of wine!

Veal escalopes: dry Italian whites such as Pinot Grigio or an Italian red like Chianti.

Osso buco: Italian dry whites such as Soave just have the edge on reds, I feel.

VEGETABLES

Vegetables are no different from any other ingredient—you need to think about the way they're cooked when you're debating what to drink. They are, however, more seasonal than other foods, so the time of year may affect your wine choice.

Spring vegetables and salads e.g. asparagus, peas, and fava beans: crisp fresh, fruity whites such as Sauvignon Blanc and Grüner Veltliner.

Summer vegetables e.g. Mediterranean vegetables such as tomatoes, bell peppers, eggplants, and zucchini: dry rosés and medium-bodied southern French and Italian reds.

Autumn vegetables e.g. corn, squash, pumpkin, and mushrooms: a buttery Chardonnay goes particularly well with the first three. A lighter Chardonnay or Pinot Noir are both good choices with mushrooms.

Winter vegetables e.g. onions, carrots, parsnips, and dark leafy greens: often served in hearty dishes such as stews and soups, tend to suit rustic reds and ales.

Vegetarian dishes: vegetarian bakes that contain beans or cheese again suit hearty reds, but you will need to check that they

are suitable for vegetarians (i.e. that no animal-derived products have been used in making them.)

CHEESE

Red wine isn't always the best choice with cheese, as I explain on pages 136–138.

Goat cheese: Sauvignon Blanc and other dry whites.

Camembert and Brie-style cheeses: fruity reds such as Pinot Noir and Merlot. Hard cider is particularly good with Camembert.

Cheddar and other hard cheeses: aged Spanish reds such as Rioja.

Strong washed-rind cheeses such as Epoisses and Munster: strong Belgian beers work better than wine, although Gewürztraminer is a classic pairing for Munster.

Blue Cheeses: sweet wines, port, or sweeter sherries.

Hot cheese dishes: white wines generally work better than reds, unless it's a baked pasta dish like lasagne. With a fondue you need a really crisp, dry white like a Chasselas from Switzerland. With a macaroni and cheese, try a light Chardonnay.

DESSERTS

You may not always want to serve a dessert wine, but there are some luscious pairings to experience.

Apple, pear, peach, and apricot-based desserts: simple French-style fruit tarts are the perfect foil for a great dessert wine like Sauternes. Apricot tarts work well with sweet Muscat.

Strawberry and raspberry desserts: need light, lemony dessert wines with good acidity like late-harvest Sauvignon and Riesling. Strawberries can be macerated in a light, fruity red wine such as Beaujolais.

Lemon-flavored desserts: can be tricky,

especially if intensely lemony. Very sweet German and Austrian dessert wines tend to work best. Serving cream with them helps.

Light, creamy desserts e.g. sponge cakes and pavlovas: demi-sec Champagne or Moscato d'Asti.

Toffee- or caramel-flavored desserts e.g. Tarte Tatin, pecan pie: late-harvested and liqueur Muscats work well with these.

Chocolate desserts: sweet reds are often easier to match than sweet whites—see page 94 and page 145.

SPICY FOOD

Spice is not the enemy of wine that it's reputed to be so long as you avoid wines that are very tannic. It's only really hot chiles that cause a problem.

Mildly spiced dishes including Middle-Eastern mezze and mild Indian curries: simple, crisp fruity whites and dry rosés work best. *See also Lamb Tagines.*

Moderately hot curries such as Rogan Josh: Inexpensive fruity New World reds such as Cabernet-Shiraz blends. With chicken curries try a Semillon-Chardonnay.

Hot curries: Tricky but try Gewürztraminer or Pinotage. Otherwise stick to lager or the Indian yogurt-based drink, lassi.

Smoked pepper, paprika, or pimentón-based dishes such as Chile con Carne, Goulash, or bean dishes flavored with chorizo: Soft, fruity reds such as Rioja, other aged Spanish reds and Zinfandel.

Thai salads and curries: better with whites than reds. Alsace Riesling and Tokay Pinot Gris work well, as does Gewürztraminer especially with red Thai curries.

matching food to wine

Sometimes the starting point for a meal is not a menu but a wine: a treasured bottle that you've been looking for an occasion to drink, a gift that you want to share with the donor or simply a serendipitous find that inspires you into the kitchen. Of course, you can enjoy it with many of the recipes in this book, particularly those in the Fine Wine Dinner (see page 130) but here are some lists of ingredients and dishes that will flatter good wines:

WHITES

Chardonnay: Lighter styles such as Chablis and good white Burgundy are perfect for simply prepared broiled fish such as plaice, dover sole, or salmon, or delicate shellfish like scallops or shrimp. Richer Chardonnays are fabulous with roast or sautéed chicken or veal, especially with wild mushrooms, with creamy or buttery sauces or with rich-tasting fall vegetables like squash and pumpkin.

Sauvignon Blanc: Unoaked Sauvignon is perfect for healthy, fresh-tasting fish dishes such as grilled sea bass, spring vegetables, especially asparagus, and goat cheese. Oaked Sauvignons, especially those that are blended with Semillon as in Bordeaux, work with similar dishes to Chardonnay.

Riesling: Dry rieslings are shown off best by delicate seafood like fresh crab, shrimp, and lightly smoked fish such as trout or salmon. Slightly sweeter styles are good with duck, goose, and subtly spiced fusion dishes with Asian influences.

Pinot Grigio/Pinot Gris: Like other dry Italian whites, Pinot Grigio is a good choice for antipasti and seafood-based pasta or risotto and simply broiled fish. Richer Pinot Gris, which often has a note of sweetness, works better with lightly spiced chicken and pork dishes, especially if given a South-East Asian twist.

Viognier: Works with similar dishes to Chardonnay, especially chicken, but can handle a little more spice.

Gewürztraminer: This exotically scented white isn't to everyone's taste, but it comes into its own with spicy food, especially Thai and moderately spiced Indian curries. It's also good with duck.

REDS

Pinot Noir e.g. red Burgundy: Duck is almost always a great choice with young fruity Pinot Noir as is simply roasted chicken and turkey and seared tuna. Older Pinots are good with guinea fowl and game birds such as pheasant and partridge.

Cabernet Sauvignon, Merlot, and blends of the two e.g. red Bordeaux: You can't go wrong with roast beef or lamb, a good steak or some simply broiled lamb chops. If you're dealing with an older vintage, keep any accompanying sauce and vegetables light—the natural meat juices are the best accompaniment.

Syrah/shiraz: French Syrahs such as those from the Northern Rhône are again good with red meat, but can take more robust treatment—intensely flavored winey stews, for example, or meat that's been cooked on an outdoor grill. Shiraz can take even more spice.

Italian reds e.g. Barolo, top Tuscan reds like Chianti: Always best enjoyed with classic Italian food, preferably from the region. Barolo is particularly good with braised beef, game, rich pasta, and truffles. Chianti shines with Italian-style roast lamb and veal and with baked pasta dishes like lasagne.

Rioja and other Spanish reds: With the revolution in Spanish winemaking, Spanish reds are changing faster than you can say paella. The typical style used to be exemplified by Rioja Reservas and Gran Reservas with their soft, delicate fruit and gentle tannins (good with broiled lamb, game, sheeps' milk cheeses and subtly spiced stews and tagines,) but the new wave of reds can handle much more robust flavors—more like a Cabernet Sauvignon or top Tuscan red, as previously.

Zinfandel, Pinotage, and other rustic reds: These are ideal for your heartiest meals like big rich meaty stews and braises. Also good with a cheeseboard.

Sweet wines: Top dessert wines like Sauternes are at their best with simple fruit tarts, especially apple, pear, peach, or nectarine-based ones and strawberry tarts with crème pâtissière (cream helps to show off sweet wines.) You can also drink them with foie gras or other rich liver pâtés and with blue cheese (the latter also being the classic way to enjoy vintage port).

Champagne: Champagne is a surprisingly flexible partner for food, particularly eggs and seafood and also handles Asian cuisines well, especially Chinese and Japanese food. A glass of sweet (demi-sec) Champagne is also a glamorous way to finish off a special meal—it goes well with light sponge cakes and other celebration cakes. *See Food and Fizz, page 113.*

frequently asked questions

WHAT SORT OF WINE GLASSES DO I NEED?

Ideally, it's useful to have four different types—a generously sized wine glass for red wines, a smaller one for white wines, a set of tall Champagne flutes, and a set of small glasses for sherry, port, and dessert wines.

HOW LONG DO I NEED TO CHILL WINE FOR?

It depends on the wine. Most people tend to serve white wines too cold and red wines too warm. Champagne and dessert wines need chilling longest (about 1½–2 hours, depending on the temperature of your fridge,) crisp dry whites need about about 1–1½ hours, full-bodied whites and light reds about 45 minutes to an hour. Even full-bodied reds benefit from being served cool rather than at room temperature (about 60–65°F), so keep them in a cooler area before serving.

HOW MUCH WINE SHOULD YOU POUR IN A GLASS?

Don't fill it more than two-thirds full. Not out of meanness, but so that you can appreciate its aromas.

HOW LONG SHOULD I OPEN RED WINES BEFORE THE MEAL?

Its only worth opening them ahead if you're going to decant them. Otherwise not much air can get into the bottle. Most wines are designed to be drunk direct from the bottle these days.

WHEN SHOULD I DECANT A WINE?

Only when it's very full bodied and tannic or has thrown a deposit like vintage port. Be careful about decanting older reds. If they're very old and fragile, they may lose their delicate flavors when exposed to air.

HOW DO I DO IT?

Leave the bottle upright for at least 24 hours before you plan to serve it (so that any deposit can settle.) Then, with a light behind the neck of the bottle, pour slowly and steadily into the decanter without stopping until you see the sediment inch towards the neck of the bottle.

HOW DO I TELL IF A WINE IS CORKED?

If it tastes musty or stale, there almost certainly is something wrong with it and you're perfectly within your rights to reject it (so long as you don't drink half the bottle first!) If it's simply too sweet or too sharp for your taste, then you've got no real grounds to send it back. The gray area is with older wines or ones made from less common grape varieties which may have funky flavors that aren't to your taste. But if a supplier or restaurant values your goodwill, they will replace it.

IF I'M INVITED TO DINNER SHOULD I TAKE A BOTTLE AND, IF SO, WHAT TYPE?

It depends how well you know your hosts. If you don't know them well, you don't want to imply that they won't serve you a decent bottle, so it's better to take something indulgent like a bottle of Champagne or a special dessert wine that could be construed as a gift. With good friends it's fine to ask what they'd like you to bring or what they're making so that you can choose something appropriate.

HOW MANY BOTTLES SHOULD YOU TAKE?

It depends on the numbers. For four of you one is fine, although if you're cautious by nature you could always take a back-up in case one is corked. For six or eight people you might want to take two (it's better to take the same type so that everyone gets a chance to try it.)

SHOULD YOU OPEN THE WINE YOUR GUESTS HAVE BROUGHT?

The trickiest issue I find! It depends how it's presented. If they bring along an unchilled bottle of Champagne, I think it's fair to accept that it is intended as a private treat to enjoy on another occasion. If they produce a bottle that they're clearly excited about, the indications are that they want to share it with you.

useful web sites

WINES, SPIRITS, AND BEVERAGES

www.matchingfoodandwine.com
My own web site with detailed recommendations on matching wine and other drinks with food.

Sherry Lehman
www.sherry-lehmann.com
Wine and spirit store, established in 1934. Stocks over 3,000 wines by color and country, most available to order on-line.

Teas Etc.
www.teasetc.com
This small Florida company works directly with growers to provide premium-quality loose-leaf teas from China, Japan, India, and Sri Lanka. The knowledgeable staff can answer any of your tea-related questions.

Grounds for Change
www.groundsforchange.com
This family-owned coffee roasting business roasts 100% Fair Trade Organic coffee in small batches to ensure the freshest coffee possible.

GENERAL

Williams Sonoma
www.william-sonoma.com
"The place for cooks." More than 250 stores nationwide selling bakeware, cook's tools, cutlery, dinnerware, flatware, linens, food, and books—also available to buy on-line.

Crate & Barrel
www.crateandbarrel.com
More than 145 stores nationwide offering a wide selection of dinnerware, flatware, glasses, picnic accessories, table linens, kitchen accessories, plus a range of gourmet foods—also available to buy on-line.

Chef's Catalog
www.chefscatalog.com
Specialist equipment for both the professional and home cook. Timers, thermometers, mixers, pastry bags, and tips, ice cream makers, bakeware, and more.

CHEESE AND DELI

Artisanal Cheese
www.artisanalcheese.com
Shop for international cheeses, artisanal foods, and craft beers from Artisanal stores or on-line.

Dean & Deluca
www.deandeluca.com
A wide selection of gourmet foods, wines, kitchenware, cookbooks, and gifts.

Zingerman's Mail Order
www.zingermans.com
Farmhouse cheeses from around the world, estate-bottled olive oils, varietal vinegars, smoked fish, sausage, coffees and teas on a web site that's both entertaining and educational.

MARKETS AND ORGANIC PRODUCE

www.ams.usda.gov/ farmersmarkets
Farmers' markets hotline at:
1-800-384-8704
To find a farmers' market in your state, check out this list compiled by the US Department of Agriculture.

www.wholefoodsmarket.com
Whole Foods Market is the world's largest retailer of natural and organic foods, with more than 140 stores across the US and Canada.

www.eatwild.com
Eat Wild is an excellent starting place if you're looking for sources for grass-fed beef, lamb, pork, poultry, and organic dairy products.

BAKERS

King Arthur Flour
www.kingarthurflour.com
America's oldest flour company sells an array of specialty and organic flours. baking products, bakeware, and tableware. Their Baker's Store also offers baking classes for professional and home bakers.
800 827 6836

CHOCOLATE

Chocosphere
www.chocosphere.com.
The best chocolates and cocoas in the world gather in a single location at an internet-only chocolate shop called Chocosphere based in Portland, Oregon. Chocosphere offers Valrhona from France, Chocovic from Spain, Scharffenberger from the US, Green & Black's Organic from the UK, Callebaut from Belgium, and many others.

INTERNATIONAL FOODS

Kalustyan's
www.kalustyans.com
123 Lexington Ave
New York, NY 10016
212-685-3451

A landmark for six decades, Kalustyan's began as an Indian spice and specialty store and has now expanded into a comprehensive source for international ingredients of every kind, including chiles, coconut products, coffees and teas, honeys, mushrooms, nuts and seeds, oils, syrups and cordials, vinegars, and much more.

La Tienda
www.tienda.com
Authentic Spanish ingredients—jamón Serrano, chorizo, Spanish smoked paprika (pimentón), premium tuna in oil, extra virgin olive oil, Marcona almonds, Spanish wines and sherry—are available online and at a retail store near Williamsburg, Virginia.
3601 La Grange Parkway
Toano VA 23168
800-710-4304

Penzeys Spices
www.penzeys.com
The source for more than 250 herbs, spices, and seasoning mixes. To order online, or to find a retail store near you, visit their web site.

conversion charts

Weights and measures have been rounded up or down slightly to make measuring easier.

1 stick butter = 8 tablespoons = 125 g

Volume equivalents:

American	Metric	Imperial
1 teaspoon	5 ml	
1 tablespoon	15 ml	
¼ cup	60 ml	2 fl oz.
⅓ cup	75 ml	2½ fl oz.
½ cup	125 ml	4 fl oz.
⅔ cup	150 ml	5 fl oz (¼ pint)
¾ cup	175 ml	6 fl oz.
1 cup	250 ml	8 fl oz.

Weight equivalents: Measurements:

Imperial	Metric	Inches	cm
1 oz.	25 g	¼ inch	5 mm
2 oz.	50 g	½ inch	1 cm
3 oz.	75 g	¾ inch	1.5 cm
4 oz.	125 g	1 inch	2.5 cm
5 oz.	150 g	2 inches	5 cm
6 oz.	175 g	3 inches	7 cm
7 oz.	200 g	4 inches	10 cm
8 oz. (½ lb)	250 g	5 inches	12 cm
9 oz.	275 g	6 inches	15 cm
10 oz.	300 g	7 inches	18 cm
11 oz.	325 g	8 inches	20 cm
12 oz.	375 g	9 inches	23 cm
13 oz.	400 g	10 inches	25 cm
14 oz.	425 g	11 inches	28 cm
15 oz.	475 g	12 inches	30 cm
16 oz. (1 lb.)	500 g		
2 lb.	1 kg		

Oven temperatures:

110°C	(225°F)	Gas ¼
120°C	(250°F)	Gas ½
140°C	(275°F)	Gas 1
150°C	(300°F)	Gas 2
160°C	(325°F)	Gas 3
180°C	(350°F)	Gas 4
190°C	(375°F)	Gas 5
200°C	(400°F)	Gas 6
220°C	(425°F)	Gas 7
230°C	(450°F)	Gas 8
240°C	(475°F)	Gas 9

index

acknowledgments

My grateful thanks to the friends who have shared the meals in this book, especially Richard and Tracey. My love, as always, to my husband Trevor, who uncomplainingly puts up with being experimented on and the ensuing chaos in the kitchen. For my children, Will, Jo, Kate, and Flyn: here's hoping these recipes will stand you in good stead. And you, Maria, too. For my mother and mother-in-law—this is what I get up to! To all at my publishers, Ryland, Peters & Small especially, Alison, Ann, and Julia. Thanks for letting me do such a fun book. And to Steve, Peter, Annie, and Helen—many thanks for making it all look so utterly gorgeous.

The publishers would like to say thank you to all our models: Helen Trent, Ros Campbell, Adam Wilkie, Zoe Lynch-Bell, Luke, and especially baby Jake (Helen's godson). Thanks also to Anna at Maiden for the loan of beautiful homewares. For more information on Maiden's products and services visit www.maiden-uk.com.